Fighting Cancer One Patient at a Time

The Poems of Dr. Susan J. Mellette

Copyright © 2014 Peter Mellette and Susan Mellette Lederhouse

All rights reserved.

ISBN: 147827459X

ISBN-13: 978-1478274599

DEDICATION

For our mother, whose healing touch and gift of caring shines through the words she left us. May her thoughts inspire future oncologists and comfort their patients.

From her beloved husband Peter, who predeceased her:

> "Even as one remains alive to the worthy causes to which one has devoted one's life, one cheerfully accepts the transfer of their leadership to younger and often remarkedly gifted persons…with some saving humor and humility, I trust the exhortation of the great American educator, Horace Mann, 'to be ashamed to die without having won some victory for humanity' as a partial payment for the great privilege of living."
>
> {From "Some of Life's Moments" by Peter Mellette, 1990.}

ACKNOWLEDGEMENTS

To *Peter Mellette and Susan Mellette Lederhouse*, who preserved these words and brought them to light.

To *Laura Safley* and the many hours she devoted to retyping these poems so that they would be preserved.

To *Natalie Miller-Moore*, who took the time to orchestrate the effort as editor.

CONTENTS

Note from the Editor	pg. 6
The Life of Dr. Susan Jackson Mellette	pg. 9
A Day in the Life of a Medical Oncologist	pg. 39
What is an Oncologist?	pg. 42
Footprints on the Sands of Time	pg. 44

Poems

A Doctor's Life	pg. 46
A Personal Life	pg. 67
Patient Relationships	pg. 78
Setbacks	pg. 98
Triumphs	pg. 112
Thoughts on Death	pg. 123
A Career in Medicine	pg. 143
On Writing	pg. 148

The Legacy of Dr. Susan Mellette	pg. 156
Scholarships in Honor of Dr. Mellette	pg. 163
About This Book	pg. 165

NOTE FROM THE EDITOR

Dr. Susan Mellette's children, Susan and Peter, undertook this book as a way to ensure their mother's work lived on. Her work as a physician leaves a legacy in the minds of those she touched, including her colleagues, her students, her patients and their families. But her children wanted to make sure that her thoughts and poetry lived on as well.

As I worked my way through more than 500 journal entries and poems from Dr. Susan Mellette, I gleaned a few things about the woman who wrote them; someone I've never met but have come to admire very much. She began her career in a time when cancer care was like throwing darts blindfolded, but Dr. Mellette's philosophy was to care for the person despite whatever odds they might be facing. She saw through the patient in the hospital bed to the heart of the individual person.

Along her journey, there are clear changes in her perspective. In her early journals from the 1960s, she struggles with the responsibilities of being a doctor and the challenges of saving lives in peril due to cancer. There are also more late night journals, indicating that the content of her days were keeping her up late. During that time, she is deeply involved with patients and their situations, as well as recognizing her own fears: her own powerlessness and how much her help is needed.

In the early 1970s, the entries reflect dark thoughts on life and death, with recurring themes of sad stories from patients and feelings of impotence in trying to save them. Dr. Mellette, at times, seems to be absorbing sadness from her patients. She reflects more on what it means to be a doctor, and seems to feel more strain on her personal life. Balancing all the tasks of caring for the desperately ill, managing hospital paperwork and politics, plus the families of the patients and the staff, are an incredibly heavy load for one person. In one entry in October 1972, Dr. Mellette quotes herself telling an intern that "the buck stops with the doctor," reflecting her philosophy of who has the ultimate responsibility.

As the journals move into the 1980s, the focus of her strong emotions shifts to the challenges of running the department, fighting internal skirmishes and regret about the administrative weight she must carry. At this time, Dr. Mellette is running the Department of Rehabilitation Medicine and focusing more on teaching medical students. She reflects on how much has changed in the profession as she passes on the knowledge. Cancer care changed so much in the 30 years she was at the Medical College of Virginia (MCV) but the care of patients is remarkably similar. They fight death and they endure pain and discomfort, while their families bring support, denial and aggravation, often all at once.

After success in curative cancer care began to accelerate nationally (and internationally,) Dr. Mellette's significant work at MCV was in establishing rehabilitation for cancer patients. Once patients had successfully achieved remission, there was still tremendous work to do, and the design of the rehabilitation programs that Dr. Mellette oversaw were crucial in shaping a holistic recovery process. It's not as remarkable today but truly the idea of "doctor as guide" was innovative during Dr. Mellette's time, and one that she fostered at MCV with thoughtful, empathetic patient care for the whole person.

In the 1990s, Dr. Mellette prepares to let go of her roles at MCV—and it's a tough process for her. First she retires from teaching, then from seeing patients, and finally from her 30 years of reviewing medical school applicants as part of the Admissions Committee. She continues to be involved in the selection of scholarship recipients for the MCV Foundation Mellette scholarship, created by a patient's family in honor of Dr. Mellette and then donated to the foundation by Dr. Mellette. Today, this scholarship fund is known as the Susan Mellette Scholarship Fund held at the MCV Foundation.

Even when she's edging toward retirement, Dr. Mellette clings to her life's work. Her time at the hospital has made many of the people she worked with her dear friends. But she does eventually leave the hospital. After the loss of her husband, Peter, in 1993, she endures COPD and its complications. As she nears the end of her life, she thinks about all she accomplished as a doctor as she struggles with being a patient herself.

As evidence of her legacy, her archives at MCV contain many cards and personal letters from her patients. She was important and well-loved in her time and her work lives on at the Massey Cancer Center at MCV. It lives not only through the medical college scholarship, but through the legacy of placing patient care at the heart of practicing medicine. I invite you to journey with Dr. Susan Mellette through the years she fought cancer, one door at a time, one patient at a time.

– *Natalie Miller-Moore*

A sample of poetry written in Dr. Mellette's own hand, below:

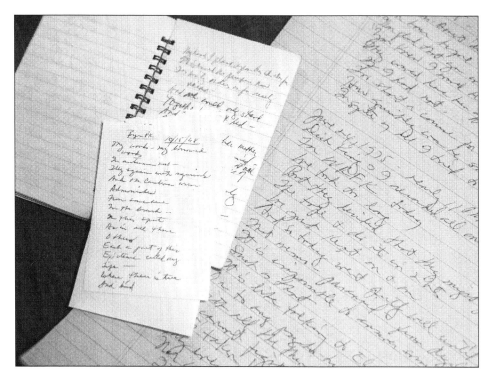

THE LIFE OF DR. SUSAN JACKSON MELLETTE

"How did I get into this? Why do I go through the torture of watching patients die – of knowing how little I have to offer in the way of treatment? Because of the "good times" – the times when a miracle was occurring – when I felt that I was doing the impossible – that I was getting the mastery over those cancer cells. Partly – and partly because those people, like those with whom I had just endured a death, need someone to share their travel and their grief."

– Dr. Mellette

It's an excellent question: How *did* she get into this? In order to understand why she undertook the heavy burden of caring for those with cancer, it's important to know the journey Dr. Mellette's life took to get her there.

Mary Susan Jackson, known in childhood to her family as "Mary Sue" and later professionally as Susan, was born June 4, 1922 in Raleigh, North Carolina. For a girl growing in up North Carolina during the 1920s and 30s, aspiring to be a doctor was not an easy career choice, but she was inspired by her family's female physician and more importantly, her own determination.

Her determination may have come in part from her parents. Her father, Donald had a law degree from Wake Forest and her mother Bessie (Mull), an A.B. from Meredith College, a Baptist school for women – it was unusual for the time for both parents to have college degrees. "They believed in making the world a better place," Susan said.

Susan excelled at school, skipping a grade because of her advanced reading skills and began junior high school (7th grade) at age 11. Due to the age difference with her fellow students, Susan had a bit of trouble making friends, but when she did find other women to connect with, they left a lasting impression on her.

Mary Susan Jackson in 1923 with sister, Elizabeth (left) and aunt, Nettie Mull

Susan Jackson in 1935, at age 13

In her journals, she talks about her first friend Anita, and Susan calls that friendship "a high point in my life." Before she moved away, Anita introduced her to Margaret, who would become one of Susan's other close friends because of their shared love of the outdoors. They pooled their money so they could buy a microscope to share. "We had discovered that we shared a common interest in the out of doors, the nature world of birds, trees, insects, etc. We began to go on 'tramps' to collect specimens or to hunt in the fields for arrowheads, then fairly common," she wrote. The microscope was their pride and joy for some years, and Susan said she spent many hours with it. Margaret, who wanted to be a surgeon, also attended medical school, and the two stayed in touch for many years.

Wherever she went, she found places and people to share her love of science and her curiosity about the world. Though it was not common for women to enter medicine, she refused to be dissuaded from her chosen career path. Here's a story to that effect: "I was at my dentist's office… and my dentist, making conversation, asked what I expected to do after graduation. Between washings and brushings, I replied that I wanted to go into medicine. He stopped his work long enough to exclaim indignantly, 'That's a bad idea. Medicine is no place for a woman. Women think they are going to be happy but they're not.' One of the things that my dentist didn't know is that I had a role model. My family physician had been a remarkable woman who had graduated from Women's Medical sometime in the early 1900s. She had been encouraged to go into medicine by her brother…My parents revered her…I can still vividly remember that feeling of relief and comfort when Dr. Carroll came for a house call."

Dr. Elizabeth Delia Dixon Carroll, the first female medical practitioner in Raleigh, and Susan's friend Margaret, who was a few years ahead of her in school, may have been her role models in seeing that her chosen path might have been unusual, but it was possible. "My interest in medicine as a career had two main roots: one was my interest in nature and thence into biology, and the other the role model which I had set for me by my family physician– one of the very early women physicians. The synthesis seemed to make sense: to use the science which I loved so in a way which could be most beneficial to others."

Through her hard work and determination, plus a strong drive for academic excellence, she succeeded. "My philosophy," she said, "I think is 'excellence' – to do the best I can each day with the capacities I have – to be the best in what I start out to do." That philosophy was first expressed in her dedication to her educational journey, which would take many years and involve many different schools.

Dr. Mellette started her college education at Meredith College, the school from which her mother Bessie Mull and sister Elizabeth graduated. She maintained a high grade point average and was active outside of class in the honor society, science club, plays and was a biology lab assistant for three years. Her senior superlative was "Most Intellectual" – no surprise there!

Peter Mellette and Susan Jackson in 1942

After completing Meredith College, she was granted a research assistantship at the University of North Carolina in Chapel Hill to do research and take medical school classes.

While visiting her sister at Crozer Theological Seminary near Philadelphia, Susan Jackson met a theological student named Peter Mellette. They were engaged within a week of meeting. "He shared my dreams," Susan explained. They were married June 16, 1943, a year after they met.

At the time of their wedding, he was still in seminary and she had just begun medical school. They spent many years on their respective educations, as she said, "It was something we did together." Between the two of them, they'd go on to obtain two more degrees for Peter after seminary, including a doctorate, and an M.D. for Susan. She described the cost of those degrees as "hard work and lots of extra jobs each to achieve them."

Susan "tried to be a good preacher's wife" in addition to school, internship and general practice but admits that, "Yes, I did sometimes get called out of church to go to see a patient." Her educational choices followed the geographic pattern of her husband's ministerial assignments – and sometimes he was serving more than one congregation at once.

They struggled to spend time together due to distance and the responsibilities of their jobs and education. After she spent two years at the University of Pennsylvania medical school, the Mellettes moved to Ohio and Susan finished medical school at the University of Cincinnati in 1947. Peter's congregation was actually closer to Columbus, and Susan's commute to Cincinnati meant the couple spent significant time apart during the week. Weekends were filled with church services and pastoral visits before she had to catch the 5:58 a.m. train from Columbus back to Cincinnati on Monday mornings.

Susan Mellette, one of eight women in the Class of 1947 from the University of Cincinnati's College of Medicine

As time went on, more cities were added to their journey together. She interned at the University Hospital in Cleveland, while he attended Western Reserve University for an M.A. in History. She had a residency at St. Barnabas Hospital in New York City, while Peter attended Columbia University for his doctorate in intergroup education. Susan then worked at the University of Louisville in Kentucky while Peter worked in Speed, Indiana as a minister, and she completed a post-doctoral fellowship at Koch Hospital in St. Louis while Peter began his intergroup relations work with the National Conference of Christians and Jews in St. Louis.

At each place she worked, she learned an element of medical practice that would inform her later work in Richmond. In Cleveland, she kept a brisk pace seeing patients with a variety of maladies. "My major frustration with general practice was that it was just not possible to see forty or fifty patients a day and do justice to anyone. I didn't like sewing up a cut finger and not being able to do a full physical examination; it was treating 'parts of people' and not people," she said. But added, "I do have a few babies named for me and found much of it satisfying."

In serving rural populations, she learned how to be creative in treating her patients. "I served an unforgettable several months as a physician for the Homeplace Rural Health Clinic in Southeastern Kentucky. We were eight miles from the nearest telephone and fifteen miles from Hazard, down a winding mountain road. I drove a Jeep up the creek-beds and became quite adept at swinging bridges and even foot-logs with a couple of inches of snow on them and the creek below. As the only physician in the area, I not only made house calls up the hollows and saw patients in our clinic office but also held clinics in some really out-of-the-way places. Examining a patient lying on a pew in a church turned out to be possible, if not ideal!" In her journals, she notes several of her early experiences with cancer and

Susan Mellette and her Jeep

chemotherapy, interesting in hindsight because of the lifelong work she would undertake at the Medical College of Virginia (MCV).

Although cancer today touches nearly everyone, including people without medical experience, cancer in the 1940s was still a hidden diagnosis. Susan describes her childhood experience with cancer as limited. "I remember a neighbor who'd had a cancer of the mouth and who died in spite of radiation therapy at Duke," she said.

Even as a medical student, she saw relatively few cancer patients – but she recollects one patient who made an impression on her. "There was a man with lung cancer. Before he went into surgery, he'd turned to me, a medical student, and said: "If I don't come out of this, will you call So and So?" I was a medical student, secure in my feeling that nothing was going to happen. After surgery, in the Recovery Room, he sat up, looking just great, and asked for a cigarette, which was given to him. Suddenly, he collapsed. Wheeled back into surgery quickly, it was found that a ligature on a major artery had come loose; but it was too late. And I didn't remember the name of the person he'd wanted notified. I assumed that the social worker did. But it was an unsettling experience."

Susan Mellette, circa 1947

Susan also recalled seeing some interesting developments in cancer research in her part-time research lab work at the University of Pennsylvania. "We were studying the war gases, mainly in terms of possible decontamination of foodstuffs. We noticed that the rats to which we'd given some of the nitrogen mustards had a decrease in blood counts. I was just a research technician. I didn't know even just which chemicals we were using. They had code numbers. Somebody far smarter than I soon decided that if these agents made the blood counts go down, they might be useful in diseases in which the white blood counts were high, i.e., leukemias and lymphomas. And they were. The era of chemotherapy had been born. But it was years later that I learned this," she said.

While Susan continued her education, chemotherapy was in its infancy. Many in medicine were involved in a scattershot attempt to find the right chemicals to work for certain cancers, and Susan was there to witness these attempts. "One day, when I was an intern in Cleveland, a Tumor Board presentation was about a patient with leukemia who had been treated with a simple chemical: urethane. Amazingly, for a time, the high blood counts had receded. It was an exciting moment. There was, perhaps, some medical control for malignancy," she said. "I had hardly even heard of chemotherapy for cancer. That, in itself, was new – exhilarating."

Then she began to see the research in practice. "After internship, I became a country doctor, in practice with a man with an established small-town/country practice. I remember only one cancer patient in the nearly two years I was there. She was a woman with breast cancer. The drug salesman had talked my partner into giving her the drug amethopterin, one of the very earliest of the chemotherapy agents, of a type different from the nitrogen mustards. I don't think that we were even told to follow blood counts. Thus did 'community cancer chemotherapy' begin," she recalled but added, "The patient died, as she was going to anyway."

During her time in New York City, she first encountered a larger number of cancer patients, and here's what she said about that experience: "In 1949, as a resident at St. Barnabas Hospital in New York, I first became 'addicted' to the care of the cancer patient, especially the patient with widespread disease. The things we could do then were small compared to today, but it is an exciting and gratifying thing to be able, sometimes, to achieve improvement which has seemed 'impossible.' And in those situations in which we 'fail,' the loss is tempered by the knowledge that we tried, as hard as possible and that we tried to give life to the days we could salvage."

St. Barnabas in the Bronx had previously been called "The Home for Incurables," but the superintendent was not going to give up on his charges. Susan notes: "Over at NYU, Rusk (a doctor later named 'the Father of Rehabilitative Medicine') was beginning to talk about rehabilitation. It was in the post-war period; and there were plenty of veterans who needed rehabilitation. Our mentor at St. Barnabas decided other patients also needed rehabilitation; and the name was changed to 'the Hospital for Chronic Diseases.' There was, however, a leftover wing donated for cancer patients, mostly very nice single rooms with balconies overlooking the 10 acres of grounds which St. Barnabas had…My first assignment was to the

Peter Mellette, circa 1960

Kane Pavilion for the cancer patients. What an awakening. These people were there until they died. I can remember only one patient leaving St. Barnabas vertically in those days; and that was a woman with cirrhosis, not a cancer patient. The others left horizontally by way of the morgue."

Despite the setbacks, Dr. Mellette was intrigued by the challenge. "A couple of these patients who had advanced breast cancer responded to the poor treatments we had available in 1950– mainly radiation therapy and male hormones. It was a wonderful realization that there was something which we could do for patients with advanced cancer. This was 'something I could get my teeth into.' It was almost 'doing the impossible,' she said.

Peter became the Assistant Director for the St. Louis area of the National Conference of Christians and Jews in 1952. The next year, he moved to Richmond to become the director of the organization's Virginia region. Dr. Mellette needed to find a job in the area, and that's how she came to the Medical College of Virginia (MCV) in 1954. She had no stated position, but she did write a weekly column called "A Doctor Advises" for Grit, a national weekly news magazine. She had research fellowship money and offered herself to work for the Division of Cancer Studies department.

"In the late summer of 1954, I stood at the bus stop on 12th street – by the Campus Room next to a dry cleaning establishment and the old Skull and Bones then in that block. I had come to apply for a position at MCV. I watched the students, the housestaff, all the people come and go and I thought how wonderful it would be to be a part of all of this," she recalls. What she didn't know was that after so many moves, she would spend nearly 40 years at MCV.

By 1956, she was promoted and offered a position at the hospital. She partnered with Dr. Lou Leone, and their partnership in the multidisciplinary cancer program allowed it to prosper in the late 1950s.

Department of HEALTH, EDUCATION, AND WELFARE · Public Health Service
National Institutes of Health · Bethesda 14, Md.

NATIONAL INSTITUTE OF ARTHRITIS AND METABOLIC DISEASES
NATIONAL CANCER INSTITUTE
NATIONAL INSTITUTE OF DENTAL RESEARCH
NATIONAL HEART INSTITUTE
NATIONAL INSTITUTE OF MENTAL HEALTH
NATIONAL MICROBIOLOGICAL INSTITUTE
NATIONAL INSTITUTE OF NEUROLOGICAL DISEASES AND BLINDNESS
THE CLINICAL CENTER
DIVISION OF RESEARCH GRANTS

January 6, 1955

In reply refer
to: HF-4075

Dr. M. Susan J. Mellette
5236 Wythe Avenue
Richmond, Virginia

Dear Dr. Mellette:

    It is with great pleasure that I inform you that the Surgeon General has approved your application for a Public Health Service Research Fellowship, the terms of which are set forth in the Statement of Award attached. You will also find certain additional information and instructions in the Award Letter Supplement.

    We earnestly hope that you will find the tenure of this Fellowship both pleasant and profitable. If we can be of assistance at any time, please do not hesitate to call on us.

Sincerely yours,

Ernest M. Allen, Chief
Division of Research Grants

cc: Dr. Leone

The NIH fellowship letter Dr. Mellette received in 1955

*Left: the MCV newsletter, featuring a photo of Dr. Mellette
Right: a photo of Dr. Mellette taken at MCV in 1960*

*Samis Grotto representatives review investments in
cancer program with Dr. Mellette*

Part of their efforts included recruiting a number of other faculty to participate part-time in both clinical and research activities.

Dr. Mellette felt that her role at MCV would give her the opportunity to do more for cancer patients. She writes: "I was an NIH fellow in research with my mentor being Louis Leone, a Life Member of the American Cancer Society. Lou was fresh from Memorial-Sloan Kettering and we were beginning to use those remarkable agents known as "cancer chemotherapy".... It was a wonderful time. I was always sure the next agent would be 'the one.' I remember agonizing over a lung cancer patient. We were expecting a shipment of AB-l03 and his primary physician was willing to let him die in the interim. I wanted so much to give him a chance at this new agent. It did, eventually, come; and it did shrink down his tumors briefly. But, like all the other things we were using in those days, the improvement was exciting but, sadly, so temporary," she recalled.

Dr. Mellette was a superb role model, acting essentially as a one person cancer center after Leone's departure in 1959 until the program's expansion in the mid-1960s. Not only did she conduct the cancer program but she contributed greatly to MCV by her staunch efforts on the Admissions Committee of the School of Medicine, beginning this work in the early 1960s and continuing for thirty more years.

She greatly enjoyed her work, difficult though it was. "I may still see twenty or more patients as day, but these are usually people with whom I've been living and working for months or years. And patient stresses are tempered by the pleasure of working with medical students and trying to help them see that the care of patients with malignant disease is not really depressing if your goal is the realistic one of achieving the very best result you can with the situation at hand, and hopefully sharing both your humanity and medical skills," she said.

The Mellette Family, with daughter Susan and son Peter

While accomplishing all of this at work, she still managed to find time to have her two children, daughter Susan and son Peter, as well as spend time with her husband Peter and accompany him during some of his professional duties. Her community activities were mainly limited to speaking for the American Cancer Society, church groups, and some TV panel shows.

"One of the important contributions to my own practice has been the American Cancer Society. I began working with the local unit in the late 1950's– not too long after we had come to Richmond. I undertook the showing of films on breast self-examination and the need for Pap smears to literally hundreds of women in our area. The audiences ranged from a half-dozen at a coffee klatch to several hundred at some of the local industries. I became so familiar with the Joe Meigs' film on Pap smears that

Dr. Mellette with American Cancer Society representatives

I once dubbed in the sound when the audio failed to work at one of the presentations," she said.

Dr. Mellette specialized in medical oncology and cancer chemotherapy, with a focus on increased post-treatment care and rehabilitation. This interest evolved into the Cancer Rehabilitation and Continuing Care program that she founded in the 1970s. Many of the activities that developed in the MCV Cancer Center in that decade, including cancer research, cancer education and cancer patient care, were ahead of their time and today remain the standard in cancer centers.

As time when on, national interest grew in the idea of cancer rehabilitation, and Dr. Mellette was able to showcase her work. "In the early 70's, when the National Institutes of Health and the National Cancer Institute, under the Cancer Act, became interested in Cancer Rehabilitation, I took the

Dr. Mellette with American Cancer Society representatives after a presentation

fundamentals I had learned from the American Cancer Society (ACS) and established a Cancer Rehabilitation Program at our institution. The message for all of us was clear: even cured cancer patients needed help to live with the disabilities which the disease and its treatment may have caused. For many other patients, it was the prevention of disability which we could achieve. The Reach to Recovery Program was a prime example. Patients could be taught ways to prevent incapacitation, even with the old Halstead radical (a mastectomy procedure.) The concept of cancer rehabilitation has been the message which I have tried to promulgate during the past quarter of a century– and it is based on those early lessons I learned from the American Cancer Society. We are still making progress in cancer rehabilitation, both in terms of awareness of the things that can be done and in terms of psychosocial and vocational elements of this field. I am grateful for the opportunities which national ACS has offered me in these areas."

In a publication called "The Patient, The Family, and The Disease," Mellette points out that the context of the patient's life cannot be overlooked, and gives examples from her own practical experience:

"The patient's reaction to his own illness is determined by his knowledge of the impact which the disease will have on those close to him as well as on himself. Job adjustments may have to be made. Financial burdens may be accumulated. Certainly the family members, as well as the patient, have to face the threat to life itself inherent in the diagnosis of cancer."

Even those beating cancer need to be realistic about how it will change their lives, she said. "We can honestly tell many patients that the chance for cure is good but there is still that phrase 'chance for cure.' For a significant segment of patients, the physical changes associated with the disease of its treatment, for example laryngectomy or colostomy, require a change in some aspects of their lives."

The publication also talks about the then-novel idea of the impact of the family unit on the cancer patient and their ability to fight their cancer.

"Cancer is a family disease. The patient and the family interact in their reactions to cancer, employing these and other coping mechanisms. How can we as health professionals or concerned persons improve our care of the family which is so inextricably tied in with our care of the patient?" Mellette suggests three things:

- We can increase our awareness of the total family constellation.
- We can raise our level of understanding of some of these basic mechanisms of behavior
- We can increase our own adaptability

Dr. Mellette with colleagues at MCV in 1974
Photo courtesy of VA Department of Vocational Rehabilitation

These types of suggestions were revolutionary in their own way, extending beyond the patient who occupied a hospital bed and had an individual chart – it reached to their family system, to their emotional health and to the prospective future after cancer.

Another important work "The Evolving Role of Cancer Rehabilitation in Cancer Care," which Dr. Mellette presented at a cancer conference in 1994, emphasized the need to look at cancer's effects on patients as more than just physical. The side effects of treatment and the lasting changes to a patient who has successfully defeated cancer mattered enormously to her patients, and therefore, to her. In a draft of the paper, she said, "I was 'sold' on rehabilitation; but I was also 'sold' on trying to bring its benefits to cancer patients."

Her work with Patricia Franco, a paper entitled, "Psychosocial Barriers to Employment of the Cancer Survivor" in 1987 was later included in a paper highlighting the need for cancer survivors to be covered by the Americans with Disabilities Act, so they could continue to work and provide for their families.

While Dr. Mellette was intensely focused on her work, the university setting at MCV allowed for more than just treating patients. There was research, and the training of medical students– one of her main loves. In addition to her other roles, she taught students as a Professor of Internal Medicine and Rehabilitation Medicine at MCV. "One of the things I always tried to teach my students was that maxim stated so well many years ago by Dr. Francis Peabody: the secret of the care of the patient is in caring for the patient. The practice of oncology has not yet progressed to the point that we can write a prescription and expect a cure. The challenges in terms of better treatments and the need for 'caring' for the patient and his family are still there," she said. Dr. Mellette lived this philosophy and according to many letters from patients, she succeeded.

Over a 20 year period, Dr. Mellette was selected for and served on several National Institutes of Health grant evaluation committees. These committees evaluated grant applications for cancer centers, rehabilitation medicine programs and even basic research. She visited centers around the country and reviewed their requests for new and continued funding, which also gave her an excellent overview of the national landscape of cancer care. She also served a term as board president of the American Association of Cancer Education.

Along with her many documented accomplishments as a doctor, Dr. Mellette had some overlooked accomplishments as well. In a time when women doctors and oncology were quite new, Dr. Mellette was a pioneer in the field. Fighting discrimination of women in the medical field in ways such as admission to medical school and comments from male practitioners, Dr. Mellette encouraged the then-small class of female medical students and paved the way for more women to become involved in the medical field.

Dr. Mellette with her housekeeper Vincella Cross around 1980

Being a medical oncologist was rare in Dr. Mellette's early career, partly because medical oncology was not a separate sub-specialty yet. When she first came to MCV, she was one of two people in the state of Virginia treating cancer in the way that we now think of medical oncologists doing so. The achievement is not just being the first woman oncologist in Virginia - at one point she was *the* medical oncologist in the state.

Beyond her pioneering as a woman oncologist, Dr. Mellette was known for her style of patient care. Often referred to as "mother" by her patients, Dr. Mellette was the doctor many turned to for hope and compassion. She said of patient care, "Part of my job as a physician is to be there, to offer support, to help them make an adjustment. It's up to me to be part of whatever happens to my patients, certainly at this particular time. We're in this together. It's something we both have a big stake in."

Additionally, she had an exceptional career while also raising two children, Susan and Peter, and being a partner to her husband Peter, whose job often took him out of town. His role with the National Conference of Christians and Jews grew to include the Carolinas, Kentucky, and Tennessee, later adding Ohio and Indiana. In the late 1970s, he became a National Vice-President of the National Conference. In 1981, he stepped down from his Virginia directorship and retired fully in 1982. During their long marriage, Susan and Peter created a partnership built on their shared dreams, and on treating people compassionately. In 1987 they were jointly awarded the Richmond Chapter Humanitarian Award from the Virginia Region of the National Conference of Christians and Jews, now the Virginia Center for Inclusive Communities.

Susan continued working until Peter's health declined and she decided to retire from teaching and became Professor Emerita in 1992. She writes about it in her journal, "You see those last few months gave me something very real that I'll never have again in the same way – never again will I be

Susan and Peter at one of their favorite vacation spots

able to be so sure I was needed. That last 14 months was hard in many ways because I lost him little by little – but a part of him – a sweet, patient part came out then – that gave me something I'll always be able to remember. When I asked what I really had accomplished in life, I decided being a good wife to a great man was something worth doing and that I'd tried to do that – Then those last few months I was able to really be needed." Peter passed away on February 3, 1993.

It took until 1995 for Dr. Mellette to completely retire from MCV. Although Dr. Mellette struggled with her feelings about retirement, she still was able to reflect on her life's work. "It is Christmas-time, 1996. A large package arrives for me. I know what it is before I look. The sender, a successful business man, has sent a Smithfield ham every year for the past more than a dozen years. He is one of my few 'miracles.' He'd had cancer of the stomach, which had already spread to the nodes in the area. He'd been told that, at the most, he had a few months to live. I'd given him chemotherapy of a mild type and radiation therapy and, amazingly, the

The MCV Rehabilitation Center Team in the late 1980s

nodes disappeared and all subsequent CT scans and other studies showed no evidence of cancer. We'd kept up the 5FU (a chemo drug) for a couple of years – we didn't know when to stop. Now all these years later, he is one of my few cures."

Dr. Mellette notes that despite the honors she was awarded in her career, that "I didn't want honors. I wanted achievements." She was very hard on herself in looking back on her patients' outcomes, even though their cases were far in the past. "That Christmas in 1996, there was also a gift from a patient with breast cancer with a poor prognosis by the numbers. That was ten or so years ago and she's fine. Her note: 'I cherish every day of my life and I feel I owe it to you.' There were cards and gifts, too, from some families of patients with whom I'd not been successful; but they still remembered how hard I'd tried. Is this all I have to show for over forty years as a medical oncologist?"

But many of her reflections on her career indicate a great deal of hope in the treatment of cancer patients – both in the traditional sense of trying to cure them from cancer, but also in improving the manner in which they were treated by hospital staff. "A lot has happened in the years since then. We've found some new drugs and, more importantly, the value of combinations. We've found the value of adjuvant treatment. Now, all the patients seen by the medical oncologist need not be patients with advanced disease. And we are actually curing some: lymphomas, testicular cancers, and some others. It is a better day; but we still have so far to go," she said in the late 1990s.

That results-oriented focus appears to be a consistent part of Dr. Mellette's personality in addition to fierce determination, and it's no surprise that she continued to serve even after her official retirement. "Yesterday, my five year old granddaughter asked me, out of a clear blue sky: 'Grandma, now that you're retired, are you still helping people?' In the first place, I wasn't entirely aware that she was aware that that was what I considered

Dr. Mellette, with her son Peter, his wife Kerry and their daughter, Kelsey Mellette in 1994

Dr. Mellette at her retirement celebration, with Drs. Sheldon Horsley and Walter Lawrence

myself doing all these years. In the second place, it was something which I had already asked myself: 'What am I doing now which is really of help to people?' I've been finding some opportunities in serving again (after 30 previous years) on the medical school admissions committee and continuing to serve on the Cancer Education Council. It is these new ones coming along who will carry the torch for the continually improving care of the cancer patient, for the research which will uncover better treatments, for the cancer rehabilitation which will enable people to live with the effects of the cancer or its treatment until that day comes when there is, indeed, a cure."

She intended to leave a legacy of treating patients well, as people, and as individuals. Medical students, who are often eager to prove their technical skills, often need that reminder!

The MCV Foundation at Virginia Commonwealth University (VCU) continues the Susan Mellette Scholarship Fund held at the MCV Foundation for medical students interested in oncology careers, bequeathed in substantial part to Dr. Mellette by the widow of one

Dr. Mellette, with Dr. Wade Smith

of Dr. Mellette's patients. There is also a Mull-Jackson-Mellette First Family Scholarship at Meredith College (still an all-women's school) for undergraduates interested in science careers and a University of Cincinnati scholarship.

Dr. Mellette passed away at the age of 78, on September 10, 2000, from complications from a fractured hip, combined with COPD and congestive heart failure. Today, her memory lives on in the legacy she left at MCV, with her patients and their families, and her children and two grandchildren. One of her granddaughters, Margot, plans to be a doctor, just like Dr. Susan Mellette.

A pioneer and role model in the medical field, Dr. Mellette is looked up to by many people. In this book, a mostly unshared part of Dr. Mellette's life, her poetry, helps us understand the day-to-day feelings she had about her job as an oncologist.

Even during her early years in residency at a chronic illness hospital in New York, she used writing as an outlet. She took a writing class at Columbia University in the evenings "just to give me an outlet from the depressing atmosphere in which I was embroiled."

She loved to write, and in a letter to one of her college professors in 1974, she looks back and wonders if she loves one thing more than medicine: "I guess words were my first love – even ahead of science."

Peter Mellette said of his mother: "My mother was a writer. Her oncology practice and her professional and family commitments led to long working days and nights. Yet in spite of her busy schedule, she made time for something that she loved almost as much as her patients and family. Much of my mother's poetry emanates from efforts to process the sadness and stress of caring for terminally ill patients. As her outlet, her coping mechanism after a 14-hour day of patient visits and professional encounters, my mother would sit at her typewriter and let the conscious and subconscious emotions flow into words."

Please consider yourself invited to observe and absorb the words of Dr. Susan Mellette.

Dr. Mellette doing rounds at MCV

A DAY IN THE LIFE OF A MEDICAL ONCOLOGIST

Here's a glimpse into some of Dr. Mellette's daily interactions with patients and hospital staff, in her own words.

"Good news, the mass in your chest is smaller. The chemotherapy is working."

The patient extended her arms and gave me a big hug.

"Maybe it's worth losing my hair," she said. "I might just make that grandchild's graduation after all. At least with my wig."

"I expect you will" I answered. "I'm sorry about the hair but at least this is working."

I did not mention that I couldn't be sure how long this remission would last. I don't really know. The chances are a few weeks or months – but it might be a lot longer. I always think it will be. I never let myself remember the statistics. How can I know that she won't be one of those "lucky ones" who get years and not just months after treatment? I don't know for sure.

It is afternoon office hours in my medical oncology office. The next patient is a "follow up." "Everything looks fine," I say. "Just come back in a couple of months."

The next patient is another story – Deeply jaundiced, weak and shaky, this patient has advanced pancreatic cancer.

"How are things going?" I ask.

"Not good. I can't eat, I can't sleep and I still have to take those pain pills every four hours or I know I didn't."

I examine the abdomen with the protruding liver and the fluid.

"Let's see what else we can do," I say. "Your blood counts still aren't high enough for any more chemotherapy right now but we can give you some pills to get rid of some of this fluid. That might help. And it's OK to take the pain pills – Don't worry about that."

"The floor just called," interrupted the nurse. "Mr. B. is having trouble."

It's not likely that they would call unless something dire is happening. I call back.

"Mr. B's blood pressure is dropping and he's not responding well. The family is upset."

"I'll be there in a few minutes. Now let me talk with the resident."

"Mr. B's dying," says the resident. "The family didn't seem to be willing to recognize that."

"Hang on," I say, "I'll be there."

I hurriedly finished with the cancer patient, wrote a couple of prescriptions and tell them to keep me posted as to how things are going. I go through two buildings and arrive on the floor to find the situation even worse than expected.

"I knew this was coming," said the wife. "But it's just so hard."

"I know." I hold her hand a few minutes.

"Dr. J-, the resident, has just given him something for pain," the wife adds.

I know it's unlikely the patient is feeling actual pain but the medication is comforting to the family. I know that my own reluctance to do this, will merely mean a longer time to this exodus. I restrain myself from giving Dr.

J- a piece of my mind. Is there any benefit to dragging out these last few hours?

"I'm afraid we don't have anything else to offer," I tell the wife and the daughters. They nod.

"I'll be back," I say and beat it out back to the outpatient office.

Mr. B is breathing his last when I return. I stood by the bedside with the family until the last breath.

"We had nothing left to give," I say after they have comforted themselves a bit. "He put up a good fight – and you helped him. You were always there."

We finish the immediate arrangements and I see the family to the elevator. It's the least I can do. Their reason for being on the floor has ceased to exist. They are now my guests. The chaplain who had arrived a bit earlier, goes down with them. I go back to make a note on the chart and sign the death certificate for the waiting rep from the office.

"I'd treated this man for a couple of years," I say. "He was a nice person."

How did I get into this? Why do I go through the torture of watching patients die – of knowing how little I have to offer in the way of treatment? Because of the "good times" – the times when a miracle was occurring – when I felt that I was doing the impossible – that I was getting the mastery over those cancer cells. Partly – and partly because those people, like those with whom I had just endured a death, need someone to share their travel and their grief.

WHAT IS AN ONCOLOGIST?

"What is an oncologist?" they asked – in a planted question for the television panel.

And I answered: "One who specializes in lumps – In tumors or a cancer specialist: medical oncologist, surgical oncologist, pediatric oncologist."

What is it like to be an oncologist – a medical oncologist?

It is standing by Mrs. B.'s bed – having her look up at me tonight with those shining eyes and that beautiful head of steel gray hair which hasn't fallen out yet but will, in a couple of weeks. It is hearing her ask: "Am I really going to get better? I just don't think I am."

It is seeing today that R-'s nodes have gone down because I was brave enough to give him the adriamycin – knowing he'd lose the bushy beard of which he's so proud – and being grateful.

It is seeing Mary, whose family bought a hospital bed for her to go home to – in which they expected her to die – two years ago and watching her perky little walk.

It is hearing Mrs. W. exalt over the end of the two years of treatment with alkuron for her carcinoma and having to agree to stopping treatment now. And knowing that, two years ago, when I spoke of this as "preventative" I wasn't all that sure in my own mind. It is knowing that in the next exam booth is B-, whose treatment I did stop after three years – only to have the tumorous lymph nodes in his neck reappear.

It is watching Mrs. T become so weak that she is less talkative. It is looking at her X-rays and seeing an increase in the golf ball sized densities in her lungs. And making sounds to her son about the decrease in the rate of growth – and knowing that even if my medicine was working, it wasn't working well.

It is remembering Greg, the Adonis, whose life I did not even prolong – and writing with this gift pen from another with a similar tumor when I have not thanked him because I was not brave enough to tell him his chemistries are now abnormal.

It is all of these things – these people – these fears – these triumphs – these defeats. It is these I shall remember in the night in semi-vignettes – How long? A year? A month? A day? Ten years?

Footprints on the Sands of Time
March 22, 1995

Let this then be the journal of the golden days –
these likely few remaining days
in which to capture some of
the essence of a life –
a life which seemed so good
in many ways.
A life in which I may have left
some footprints on the
sands of time –
(though note that they *are* sands)
we live, we die,
we procreate –
and we are proud of what we did.
We think the products of our love
are special people – giving much.
We feel that we have left
new feet to put these footprints
in the sands of time –
we hope the work we did
has left some trace –
though most of those it touched
no longer walk the sands.
Perhaps we flatter just ourselves
that what we did was
meaningful.

POEMS

A DOCTOR'S LIFE
♋

Letter to a New Patient
March 22, 1969

"Tonight I looked into your eyes – and saw your tears
"They come unbidden," (this you said)
whenever I allow myself to think of those I love."
And thus you told me that you knew the odds we face . . .
and, in a sense, I find it better that you know –
for then we start together on this battleground . . .
for that is what it is – we know that – each of us–
but I alone can know the real amalgam that my bullets are . . .
though I could wish them golden, they are brass –
you, on the other hand, are unaware, perhaps, that even brass
may dent, sometimes, the armor of our foe;
and I am optimist enough to hope – to pray – that each small dent
may buy us room for an advance – for you – not just for those
who are to come. (We'll find their bullets as the need arise.)
It is for you we fight today – for your tomorrows – for those years
you have expected which are threatened now.
What can I promise you tonight? This single certainty
that I command: just this – that I shall choose the ammunition
that I use with care – to make the most of every weapon that we have.
of this you may be sure . . .
And one more vow I make – a corollary pledge –
that I shall not retreat – I shall be there beside you

come what may. A colleague and an ally of a sort, as well as one
who must direct the fight.
Your battle is my own as well . . . for you – and those you love
a campaign worthy of the best that all of us can give,
with due humility for those who know
the limits of their finite power, but are not unaware
that each small particle of light we have – is harbinger and proof
of greater light awaiting means – to make it
visible.

Debts Unpayable
August 14, 1974

"There is a moral obligation which I feel," I said,
"because of all the effort by the ones
who came before."
I recognize that nothing binds me to admit
their contribution then
we could go on unheeding
taking all – for it is ours –
so ordered, so ordained, by those who grant
these funds.
And yet . . .
How can we just ignore a contribution made
from which we now reap benefit –
and those who helped to put us where we are
forgotten – spurned?
Is it not then a mark
of our humanity
that we acknowledge those who gave
for us?
It matters not if their own ends were also being
served.
It seems like taking all the apples from the kid
who climbed the tree
and threw them gently down
into our waiting hands.
Or children spurning parents who had sacrificed
to give their offspring things they never had.
We never stand alone
in this our life.

We reached our present pinnacle
upon the backs of countless men
who, though they may have asked no reverence for such,
deserve it just the same.
A "moral obligation" is a greater debt
than one
which can be counted, measured, paid at last
in full.
We cannot quantitate some debts; but that does not
imply
that they do not exist . . . in fact, the opposite,
for we shall never know just when such debts
are paid.
I shuddered, for I did not feel
that she could ever, ever
understand.

The People's Doctor
April 23, 1969

How much do I really care about these patients who will die?
Enough, I think . . . and yet the day that I begin the trek with one . .
I have already often made a compromise . . . Not consciously, perhaps,
but I have drawn the limits as we always do – with anyone.
The living – or the ones who are to die . . . we think,
"This, then will be the basis of relationship . . . This much . . . No more"
How much more likely are we to define the borders for the ones
who are to die . . . and yet –
I cannot quite believe that I have ever done so consciously
At least with those still in their early course –
I have approached each day as it arose; reacted to it then
And changed my tactics when the need was there – or I could see
No other pattern for me to accept.
I surely do not think of J– or J– or R–
Or even Mrs. W. – as anything but people – as I see them now . . .
These people I enjoy – and what I do for them –
is pleasure – and a bonus – not a pawn . . .
I think I really am a "people doctor" for I cannot think
of them as "patients" – in the sense that they
exist for me in reference only to disease – the problems they present.
I often think I even half–forget
the tumor – or I make myself ignore
its ravages. A strange phenomenon is this . . .
I live – I breathe – I love the life I live – in many ways
So many ways . . .
A role I play – at times – I always have . . .
I "watch myself" as I "perform". . . I cast an image I admire
and try to function in such entity – no acting that in truth . . .
But wishing – aiming – at a better soul,

A one fulfilling all the best that there should be
In one who does the work I do . . . or one who tries to do
such work in honesty to meet a high ideal,
to search my soul – tonight – I still may try –
But how I hope for their sake – and for mine – that what I do
is a fulfillment of a sort – a valid thing . . .
That thing of which I wrote when I avowed that my initials should be linked
alone with those which stood for this: A Work . . .
for this my aim, my goal, my heart's desire.

For Those Who Treat the Crab
April 22, 1971

But, first of all, my friend physician, you
must live
alone within your skin . . . Your motives naked
as were drying bones.
defenses recognized,
exposed.
To dread the peeking in beneath facade
created for ourselves as well as for
the world.
Omnipotence is an impossible
for those who treat the crab.
We swap our healing power for other guise
"the ever-loving friend" is one.
The one who would evoke a cure – if such were possible –
the one who "cares"
today . . . tomorrow . . . endlessly . . .
This face is useful more for families
than for the patient – who most often still expects
a touch – if not the full
costume of plenipotency
(nor is it often fair to own our helplessness.)
Self-honesty requires a recognition that
there may be answers which we fail
to see . . . to know . . . and pleading
ineffectuality
may be as great a lie as "playing God."

Privilege
April 18, 1974

Another spring in Ginter Park
each year I've asked myself
How many springs am I allowed?
How many times to see
the red azaleas and the pink and purple ones
the tulip trees, the cherries, the wisteria?
These days I feel so sorry for myself at times
because I bear
the burdens of the ill . . . the catalogue of human misery
unfolds each day.
And I ask why it is my lot to spend the years I have
so constantly as the recipient for tales of woe.
Another question might as well be asked:
Why not?
If you are granted privilege to see the spring,
then make for others some small splash of color
in their lives.

Joy
August 11, 1974

Were there, somewhere, a genie who could grant
three wishes – or just one,
the choice an easy thing – for one or three:
"To those who suffer, those who mourn
To all of those I touch,
Let me bring
Joy: the greatest of the great
Intangibles."
For "comfort," "peace," "serenity,"
though good – are not enough,
they are not positive enough;
they represent all static planes,
all high plateaus, not peaks.
For towering above them all is a pinnacle called
Joy.

Drawing Strength
August 19, 1974

From Monday on through Thursday, what a week!
This week I took to tend to "paper work"
to struggle with the contract – and to try to be
Administrator – as it says I am.
Each day became more bogged – less livable.
Each day I felt as though I was a pawn
upon the hand of Fate – prognosis poor –
No reason to exist – and little wish . . .
"Vacation" from the patients it was meant to be
as well.
A "breathing time" and one which might
recover soul.
Today I reached conclusion inescapable
I could not even straighten out my thoughts
I could not go on as I was with budgets, words,
more memoranda – or the like . . .
And so I said to him who was to work for me
"Don't bother now, I'll see my own today."
I had to see my patients, not for them alone,
but for myself . . .
And great discovery – it worked –
Tonight I have more energy to do the things
which had begun to seem impossible.
My patients give me reason to exist –
they are for me, my "tangible."
And though I know, and far too well, how much they take,
the strange reality is this:
they are, as well, my source of
strength.

Our Best Version
February 12, 1974

And finally – after all these years
of wondering why it was I had rapport
with patients and did not feel need
to ask about their inmost thoughts – their psyche,
their entanglements – their mother love – or lack of it –
rebelled almost against the revelations which could come –
allowed the opportunity but did not ask
the probing questions which might be the ones
to give me "insight" into whys or hows . . .
And often felt a guilty pang because
I did not so inquire.
Now I begin to see
my patients like me just because of this
because I let them be
the version that they want to be in my own eyes,
the idealized version of themselves – whate'er that be.
I do not make them recognize their faults,
face up to life and all the ills it holds
I let them get away with fantasy – if that is what
they want.
I never scrape away the covering
though I may see beneath.
I never let them know I also know their faults . . .
I let them be the children playing house.
I play along as though they were
the "Mrs. Smith" or "Mr. Jones"
of childhood fantasy.
I let them play at Tarzan or Jane . . . I do not prick
the bubble of their pride – their self–sufficiency

though feigned . . . I okay along with them
as though it all were real.
Is this the secret of a sort of a success?
I think I have success –
I seem to merit overweening confidence.
Is it because
They trust me not to make them face the truth . . .
We play a game – together – And why not?
When life is all too short it might as well be "fun."
I tell them they are wonderful – and so they are –
I see their best – and not their worst
And do not try to see that side –
I ask no confidence – demand no vows.
I give to them acceptance not just as they are
but as their version of their best –
The persons that they really think they are
or want to be.

Hopes
December 13, 1973

To act or not to act?
To wait and merely hope
That some great revelation will come down
And give the answers that are veiled as yet
A valid plan? Or merely just another way
To make procrastination seem a therapy?
The activists dash in – tap chests (traumatically)
Write discharge orders (Thus removing problems from
Their sight.)
And I . . . I bide my time . . . against the day
I'll find the answer that I want for this one day
This one more time, perhaps,
To stay advance
Of tumor for this patient lying there.
I always hope, I know, for miracle
(Sometimes it almost is)
Sometimes the doomed have respite for a while
At least.
And I know joy.
At other times, there is no evidence
That either waiting – or proceeding –
Changed a course.
"I'm not so dumb," said Mrs. W.,
"I can see what's going on. I want just one more Christmas
Spent in Jersey with my friends."
I tried to tell her she need not suppose
That such an end approached – so soon –
And then I looked at X–ray films
And railed against the Fate

Which made them worse – not better –
When I'd dared to hope for more.
Is it the trust they have in me which makes it hard
To recognize decline?
I doubt that this is all.
I want so much for them – and seemingly –
Have little – so, so little which is good.
Nor do I seem to have the brains to make
Discoveries which can change advance of doom.
And thoughts I'd had and hadn't followed up
Sometimes were used by others to achieve a goal . . .
And plans that now I use,
Evolved from other brains . . . and I,
The follower alone.
And yet . . . I know I still expect . . . That someday,
Some way, some great brainstorm will evolve
Fortuitously, perhaps, but potently
To add one brick at least unto that structure which should be
The "Cancer Cure."

Unintentioned Ineptitude
April 10, 1975

If, as I have averred, there is release
In poetry . . .
Then let it work its art
For me, this moment . . . now
This moment of depression – loss of zest
This hour of searching soul
And liking not
What I find there.
Self-consciousness – Yes, some of that . . .
But more: This feeling of ineptitude
The thought that I
Have failed to meet the goals I set
For me – this image that I cast
This loving person, going down the
Second mile.
Instead I find myself
An unavailable – Prevaricating
Unintentioned – but still true.
I promised I would call that doctor and I failed.
I never got around to doing that – or other things
The basic necessary things.
For the energy to do – to give – to be
Was just not there.
Nor is it now.
Nor do I seem to have the hope
It can be found.
Why do I feel dissatisfied
With what I did today
Because I read the same old verse again

Because I saw the lady sitting there
Whose letter I had just ignored.
Because I'd not lived up to all
That they expect.
Far better to be nothing than to have
Myself proclaimed a saint
When I keep failing like the devil
That I am.

Little Triumphs
July 19, 1972

How long endure the knowledge that I cannot really change
The course of the disease for most of those
I treat.
How long stand by and make my feeble jabs
At hanging on for this one and for that . . .
And feel my heart begin to break as they get worse
While everything I do is proving valueless.
To watch M- try to walk erect
So bravely fight to keep her home unchanged
Her children happy, unencumbered by her weaknesses.
And Mrs. C., jaundiced, haggard, barely here –
What use am I when I cannot reverse
Such trends.
What chances to improve their status am I missing now?
Is there some knowledge I have not imbibed
Which might be used effectively?
When both the older Mrs. K's are doing well
For now . . . Does this make up
For the third one who may obstruct one day
Not too far distant if the trend is not reversed?
What justice is there when the ones who have so much to give
Respond so poorly to the treatments that I have?
And yet . . . Of those I've seen this week – there is enough
To comfort one: When Mrs. W. can walk again –
And has no sign of any new disease – a sort of triumph this.
And Mrs. S. – fighting with the beauty and the will
Which are combined her trademark – she the optimist –
And her improvement almost still a miracle . . .
The masses gone entirely for Miss C. – although

Her ninety years – do make a difference in her total state.
And Mrs. B – all radiant – and feeling well – she says
A year and better now – again – a sort of miracle . . .
R- . . . whose family expected her to die almost at once
Not inching one arm or one leg but jumping up almost . . .
So far, so good . . . for her.
D-'s hard to quantitate . . . her status not too bad
Considering. It surely could be worse.
And Mrs. C. came from gross hemoptysis two years ago
To tell me of her 80 year old beau.
But Mrs. A. may be skating on some ice too thin for peace
A giving woman – and a solid one – another magic pill we need
For her.
E- is another who is barely stabilized. Her lungs a bit
Too fuzzy to enhance one's confidence – but working and still
Planning on vacation trip (Let's get this in at least . . .)
Then Mrs. P. who's had remission excellent – thus far –
And may again.
G- . . . no fair trial . . . but a most unlikely one.
R- . . . the joy of these last years . . . a one to make
The failures bearable . . .
So what have I to weep about – when 6 of 10 have gained
At least a respite more than average – a really worthwhile stretch
Perhaps in those great days which still must come
There will be ways to keep their ships afloat – and under sail
At least. It is worthwhile to try . . . The failures cannot cover up
The little triumphs which are ours today –
and must be harbingers – of more.

The Return
July 5, 1972

A week and a day
Away from this work –
And it seems a year –
Contact lost in seven days?
How rapidly –
Can we dissolve the bonds
That hold us to the duty
And the joy?
Returning is a sort of joy
My parish this –
For jealous am I of each one
Allegiance is a sacred thing –
If I expect –
Devotion – loyalty –
Then should I not require
This of myself as well –
Am I entitled to the days away . . .
When problems do not wait . . .
Thus it was I who stopped the fluids now.
Who yielded to the pressure they applied –
Who had not been there
All those days before
Of coma which had supervened
6 days ago –
Thus it is I who make
Decisions now –

The positive – the negative
The in-between –
The buck stops here.
This price I pay
For playing God.

Miracle
February 28, 1975 10 A.M.

Another miracle . . . another day . . .
another day to live, and breathe, and work
To see the miracles we have contrived . . . With our technology.
To know the love of fellow human hearts
Another miracle much greater than the buildings, bridges, or machines.

A PERSONAL LIFE

Peter's Birthday
July 3, 1975 – 12:15 P.M.

And in another 20 hours or so it'll be
The birthday of my son – my lovely son
For whom I have not bought a thing
I've been depressed today . . . last night I hurried home – frustrated as I was
And went to bed. Tonight I worked at making slides – and feeling hopeless
For the days have flown . . . I have allowed no time – no time at all
To get these things all done – And now – instead of having something
Wonderful. It will be mediocre – and what can I do
To make it otherwise?

July 3, 1975 – 7:45 P.M.

I tried so hard to make it home– for Peter's birthday dinner– But
As usual . . . I failed . . . Why must I always be so hard on me?
That's easy . . . I deserve it . . .
for I cannot set Priorities.
And on tonight, just when I would have gone on home,
Mrs. D. "went to pot"
With hypertension – and I had to go . . . To see what I could do
My efforts weren't worth much I fear – not even in the lesser role –
of holding hands.
My problem is – I feel I know so little and I do not like to be exposed
As ignorant. Someday I hope I'll learn. I wish that I could learn.

A Vacation
August 26, 1974

How can I say I care when I have not been near
Their beds – for two whole weeks –
When I have done the other things that pushed
And left my patients to my colleagues' skill
How can I say I care?
I do . . . though it may seem a
Paradox.
I care just as I care for those two children of my own
The nights I do not see them for the patients take
The time there was.
I do not love my children less because I am away
Nor do I care the less about the patients
Though I see them not.
And even those who died within those days
When I was here – and yet was not with them –
If I had thought that one small thing I did
Would work a cure –
Would break the cycle of
Decline.
I would have gone . . . I did not think it would.
Acceptance of the state that was I'd made
As had the ones who stood beside those days . . .
I would have liked to stand beside as well
Because I cared
But I could not – Not that and also do the
Other things.
Eternally we stand before the cross-roads, knowing that
The choice must be for one alone
And we can only beg for wisdom, prudence, skill
To choose right.

Out of Arms
June 29, 1975 A.M.

I'm on my way to MCV at this ungodly hour
We should have let the phone ring on – since I wasn't on call.
The time was very inappropriate
For I left Peter's arms to make this trip
This saying that the patients had to take
The precedence
It doesn't matter who's on call
They still can read the name upon the chart
And leave it to a family – particularly this family –
To call me first.
In recent years it's been a whole lot easier
There have been fewer calls at night
And only rarely have I had to make
A trip like this
They make them every night
But I so seldom do . . .
And now it's nearly 3 A.M.
And I am going home – thought I am feeling unsure
About the care she'll get
How great it used to be on the Floor
There were a group of nurses one could trust, not now
They seem a bunch of idiots
It's hard to tell which one is really taking charge
The Floor of other days
Has now become St. Philip – on ward B
A shame it is to see this happen and to know
There is
No – nothing terrible –
And now with weekend shot, I'll be too tired
To even function on this day.

Yet I Still Must Go
June 29, 1975 1:30 P.M.

"And now goodbye to you, Dr. Mellette," he said
My husband who was feeling slighted when I left
On this purportedly, my Sunday
"I have to go" I said, Their father was doing good –
Their world was full and rich – and now –
It's ashes, dust . . .
I have to go –
Because they've had these weeks of hell
And more to come.
"But can you give them back their world?"
He asked . . . I stood a moment guilty, then said
"No, I cannot – I know that I cannot
And yet I still must go."
Why is it that I go?
Because they need someone to share –
Although I cannot really alter things
It is my job to try – And though I'm failing
Or, perhaps, because I can
I have to be there – just to try to salvage . . .
It is my job – but more –
It is the least that anyone can do and still
to be – a human being
In the body of
Humanity.

Thanksgiving
November 28, 1991

What a wonderful day is the day of thanks
No gifts required – no Christmas tree to trim.
No need to carol – or to plan for months ahead
A quiet day – for family –
To savor all the goodness of the year
A happy day – for us – for we are fairly well
No doom descends at this small moment
In our lives –
For doom delayed for all that is so good
My thanks – eternal thanks –
For grace and good and God
Above us all.

Susie's Graduation Day
May '75

The dinner made a fitting ending to the day
Young Peter – looking so tall and . . .
Was happy for he'd talked to Bud –
He'd never in his life yet had
A conversation with his Uncle Bud
I was so tired today – so overwhelmed
By spending all my time with people
Never having moment which was mine . . .
I really need the quietness – the time
So much of what we did today required
A patience which I did not have
Sitting – standing – listening
Being next to people all the time –
It's good to have this drive home all alone
And I am almost home
There are the blinking lights of W – LEE
Where Susie and I always clasp each other's hand
As though we're coming into some strange city
That we've never seen before –
We see the sign which says
That this is Richmond – and we ask ourselves –
What would we think of it – if it weren't familiar
If one were looking it as just one more city
Of the many that we've seen –
It is that sort of empathy with Susan which provides
Such joy – How beautiful she is

Her cheeks all flushed with pride –
With pleasure in all the events which were
This day.
For Susan has enriched our life
. . . She knows.
Has passed another milestone in her life
She is as of today, a sweet girl.

Monday Morning
November 10, 1975

There may be no one who has quite so much as I
For which
One should be glad and grateful.
I live in comfort – in a decent home
With Bennie there to do the daily tasks
I come down stairs to find my breakfast cooked,
The morning paper there to read
A cheerful spot to sit
I leave my home to go to do a work which I enjoy,
Which is a useful work – and one for which I garner
Mostly praise.
I have a husband, handsome, recognized, as an achiever
In his work . . . who was just made vice-president.
Phi Beta Kappa is my daughter, and a lovely girl,
With all the goodness and the real concern
That anyone could have.
My son is bright; and talented, and has just called to say
He has been made a prefect at his school – the highest of the honors
That they give.
I drive my car in comfort down the street . . .
It is an old car, true; but I could buy another if I wished.
And all the things that people think are needful
Can be mine so easily.
Three television sets, five radios, three cars between us,
And a mountain home as well as this in town
We are respected, recognized, in this the city where we live.
How many people have so much
I would not change my life with anyone.

How Great
April 22, 1972

How great – how very great it is
To be alive
To know that one is loved
And that one has love to give
And objects for that love.
How great – how very great to have another spring
Cold April rain and "dogwood winter"
Yellow tulips – and those red
To have eyes to see such wonders
And to know that one is glad.
How great – how very great
To have a role
In meeting basic needs
Deep human needs – for succor and support
How great to know that one has skill – and love – to give.

Time to Think
April 17, 1969   10 P.M.

The sheer and unaccustomed luxury of time to call my own amazes me . . .
Not that my work is current . . . It is not . . . Nor have my patients all
Been seen today. But it is so unusual and amazing to have time . . .
For thinking – or for working on a paper or a presentation
sometime other than
The night before it may be due.
And most of all, there is the hope that soon –
There shall indeed be time – to keep the notes in order –
And to do those things I have not done
In all these dozen years. There never was such hope before . . .
I find it hard to think – that I might find some liberty
From being pushed – harassed – compelled – and driven by the "musts"
What bliss – what joy – I might have time to see my children –
And to spend an evening in my home –
How strange – how unbelievable – would be such luxury
I might have time to write those papers
And to savor such – not pushed for deadlines long since past . . .
I really am unable to imagine such a life
So long . . . So long . . .
Has passed since such was true.
To "live again"
How strange . . .
How very wonderful . . .

Hands
August 19, 1976

Sitting in my chair, thinking of nothing, I look at my hand
And see
My mother's hand.
My index finger curving slightly as hers did
Though hers more red and gnarled a bit with washing sheets
And even milking cows.
She is gone – years since; but her finger remains
On me.
I look at my daughter's face and see
My own at twenty-one
Fresh, glowing, filled with joy of life.
I walk to the mirror and see
Not myself – whatever – whoever that is
But a fragment – mere link in that chain
Transmitter genetic – bearer of that
Which was and which will be
Its element finite – fragmented – temporal
Personal – impersonal – eternal.

PATIENT RELATIONSHIPS
♋

An Open Letter To My Patients And Their Families
March 17, 1968

Please don't "give up" until I indicate you should
Or then must– or might as well.
I don't deny that you should be "prepared"
But don't pick out the shroud– or sell the car
For when you do– the fight is lost.
And though it seems to prove that you were right
And all the hope I had was false
It may be just the opposite.
I have too long stood by the bed
I know too well the limits of my art
And when, in that rare case, I feel the end
Need not arrive as yet– that there is still
A drug– or drugs– which might give respite
For a while . . .
Believe me, please,
Too often I must also greet the end
With joy, that misery is over and release
Has come.
How can I tell you when I still have hope?
How can I make you know I am sincere?
For I am sure you think I whistle in the dark
And that I do it but to keep your spirits up.
And that just is not true; but how are you to know?
Each time it is a "first" . . . you cannot really read
My thoughts. And all my words are blurred

By that which you expect
From all the others you have known about or seen.
But they were different– they were not you
And it is this and this alone I see.
I know that I must fail . . . eventually . . .
But, O, dear Lord, not now, not yet
Not please, until I have exhausted all the stock
Of medicines – of remedies I know.
If these indeed were given to my hand
For use as the embodiment of Healing Power
Then must I wrestle as did Jacob then
Or else lament like Job– or in a later day
Yet like another beg that "this cup pass."
And fortify my begging with the plea
That it is not for me – or mine – directly – that I ask.
And if the answer still is "No"
I have no recourse but to yield
With grace . . . with recognition that I too
Am protoplasmic form.
But there remains for me a solace none
Can take away – the knowledge that I shared
With him – with her – with all of those
Who walked into the Valley of
The Infinite.

Without Permission
(no date)

She was a simple soul – I'd gathered that
The day I saw the patient at the first
"I never saw a woman doctor anywhere before,"
she said, as though I were
Some sort of freak (perhaps I am) –
And then – they'd called to say she was
Hysterical –
(A day or two had passed since he'd come in)
And when I reached the floor, she grabbed me
Begging me – "Just make him well –
Don't let them tell me he's so sick –
He just can't be" –
She'd then calmed down a bit the
Next few days – He'd stabilized
And all seemed under fair control –
Although that final day – he'd been too sick
To talk – the oxygen –
Had made but little dent …
And then –
The nurse came running down the hall –
I went – and he was motionless
No heartbeat heard – no breaths –
(The wife was sitting there)
"He made a funny noise a bit ago," she said –
"I thought I'd let him rest"
We worked upon his chest to no avail
I turned to her – assuming she could see
The obvious –
"He's going to be fine now – isn't he?"

She asked –
And I astounded answered, "No –
I'm sorry, but he's gone" –
She ran and beat upon his face
Beseeching him –
"Oh A-, talk to me"
His face was turning livid and his jaw agape
"You mean he's dead?" she screamed
"He just can't be – he didn't tell me
That he was so sick" –
She ran to get the phone to call her son
Her words: "Come quick for A-
Will not talk to me – the doctor
Says he's dead!" –
She would not leave his side
She rubbed his face –
And ran her fingers over every crease and groove –
She tried to make his jaw stay up –
And over – over – more –
"He didn't tell me that he was so sick
He just can't die without his telling me" –
It was almost as if she'd thought
He'd call to her and say –
"I have to die now" – just before he did
She seemed to think he'd let her down
By not announcing his demise aloud
She knew, we thought, the hopelessness
We'd recognized for two long months –
But she had been unwilling or unable

To accept
That the strong arm on which she leaned
Might falter and collapse –
She wouldn't leave the room –
Three hours she sat – or stood
And leaned across the bed –
Caressing busily –
But without tears –
Almost as though in trance –
From time to time I slipped into the room –
And stood beside her –
And suggested that –
She go with us into another place –
"Oh, no – Oh, no – I will not leave"
"But why – oh, why –
He can't have died –
He never told me he was going to."

How Long?
February 26, 1973

Today I broke my rule:
I told a man – a young man
And his wife
That he would likely not
Survive –
"More than six months –
If one were figuring
Percentages"
He asked for all the straight
And bitter truth –
And I obliged –
As other doctors do –
And as I say – I never will
I felt almost sadistic
As I did –
I "let him have it"
Straight and cold – He has
Two little children
And an anxious wife –
But was it fair?
What real "arrangements"
Can he make – to cushion
Blows
Like this . . .
Too late –
Too soon the holocaust
And also now too soon
He feels too poorly to do
Anything –

"I need a cigarette," he said
"I know you think I'm
Crazy to keep smoking on."
(I only wish I couldn't
Understand his need.)
I do too well –
What monster am I
That I did not cloak the doom
In fool's-gold cloth?
What purpose served?
It is the way I always did
When I refused
To set a date –
I merely said we'd work
At gaining some control –
And then . . . we'd see . . .
Is it all part of
Loss of self-esteem?
I fear it is –
If I have not the confidence
In what I am – and give
I surely can't expect
The ones to whom I speak
To have a shred of confidence
In me –
And all those years I marveled at
The confidence I seemed
To generate
In those whom I spoke
Almost without –
Awareness on my part –
And recently – this god-gift

Grace – is gone –
Or less – and I am lost
For he who said that one
Must love
Himself
As well as others spoke
A truth –
Not love of self *per se* – but self
Respect – and confidence –
Without it – there is nothing –
Nothing left but doom
For all of us.

Sale On Remnants and Day-Old Bread
April 1, 1969

For they were starving
But when offered bread
They asked for cake.
And when reminded that a bit of bread was good,
They said: "But still it is not cake"
And I agreed.
It is not really that I am "fresh-out of cake"
I do not even carry such
Among my stock in trade.
I cannot often cure.
The best that I can give
Is time – and comfort – and mere modicum of each.
Though I have begged for more
And wept at times
No fresh supplies for better sustenance
Have come into my hand.
I patch . . . make do . . . and struggle on
With that I have to give
These crumbs
These remnants of
A piece of Life.

Final Word to F.B.
Address: The Elysian Fields
March 12, 1970

It was not even brass of which those bullets were composed
Those drugs intended to control disease
Instead of gold, they proved to be but lint
Those futile feeble weapons left no trace . . .
And you are gone.
Those brave shrill words I spoke – and wrote
Those self-exalting claims . . .
They ring like wind-chimes in my ears
Like crushing wads of paper in one's hands.
'Twas there the sounding brass – the tinkling tin.
I meant them well. I ventured – but I failed –
I even failed to justify the claims I made . . .
So little respite was there in the sure advance
Of those wild cells we cannot yet control.
What secret lies submerged – unfathomed – far below
Our poor ability to comprehend?
So on . . . and on . . . and on . . . we muddle as we may
It is not wish nor will nor even sacrifice
Which makes us fail –
no lack of any one of these pertains.
It is our ignorance – our bleak stupidity
How long? How long? How long?
This soul-defeating maze?

Postscript (to FB)
June 3, 1970

Those words I wrote the twelfth of March I read again
For the first time . . . tonight . . .
And all I found was bitterness
The loss I felt that night . . . unmitigated was . . .
My medicines had failed
My wrestling with the Angel was as naught.
I could not reconcile myself to Fate
I could not own a God who let you die . . .
Not only you . . . but all the others for whose need
No really valid answers yet exist . . .
This bitterness I had to sublimate
I had to face each day those souls who looked to me
For – help – whatever shred of help that I could give . . .
And I remembered – for I had to – for some peace of mind
The small successes and the minor gains.
The three years now for one who started out almost like you,
Her tumors shrinking once again with a new drug this week.
I do not know, in this our ignorance,
Why some respond . . . and others don't,
I only know I have to try . . . and try again . . . and yet again.
I also know the joy, the happiness, of even small success.
And thus I find the courage to endure.
But there is more . . . tonight . . . which could not find its place
Among those bitter words three months ago.
For in these weeks, so many times, I have remembered
Your shy smile . . . your busy hands . . . your hope . . . your confidence

So many things ingrained into my soul
Who watched you in those stressful days,
Intangibles can never die . . . they are transferred
To those of us who stood beside
And we are richer now because you lived.
The strength – character – the soul – you were
Does not depart as protoplasm does
It is indeed eternal – boundless – infinite.

Woman in '51

"Look," she cried, "I walk . . . I came here paralyzed
And doomed to die
'Cancer,' they said . . . 'a month, a year, who knows?'
The truth we speak . . . You would not want a lie
'X-ray', they said, 'and drugs.
May stop the thing a bit . . . But don't expect to walk again
Or lead a normal life.'"
She cried . . . then acquiesced . . .
"I won't . . .
I won't ask much of life . . . It gave me sixty years
That's more than some acquire
But then I knew my vow was false . . . I had to hope
I still could know desire . . .
And now . . . I walk."
A subterfuge it is, perhaps, a farce
A happenstance with hidden demons rife
I only know I learned through those dark days
To almost acquiesce . . . then trust
In life.

Broad Shoulders
May 24, 1977

"I get so lonely in the mornings most of all,"
She sobbed, "I feel you knew my husband
Better than you really did.
I feel so close to you sometimes.
The only things that keeps me going is
To think of you –
I know it's strange; but it just seems
That you were meant to be the one
Who would take care of me."
I shifted then the load upon my shoulders just a bit
To make some room for
This one more – who needed – really needed me –
I wondered – as I have before – just how
I got elected to this awesome role.
But I have trod this patch before
And know it is delimited by time
That if I share the rocky stretch
It will be smoother down the road a bit
And then this traveler – as those before –
Can walk alone – or likely find another who
Will journey on beside – Then gently, quietly –
I may withdraw and find that then
I am not even missed.

A Day of Sadness
October 11, 1989

This day has been one myriad of sad events – a holocaust of sorts
The impotence I feel must overwhelm at times
The little that I do – when I would do so much – if I but could
Encompasses – engulfs – and leaves me feeling like a fake
For L-'s breast is raw and oozing some – although her lung is good
The medicines I give are impotent as well. Thus be it – for at least,
They do not make her worse.
And Mr. S. was squirming with his pain – the liver, maybe,
And the combination that I used – had taken down the swollen arms
But left the rest untouched – just why I do not know.
E- was just fine today – and yet, that CEA
From the last visit was increased and I am worried that
She may have new disease somewhere – while she insists
She'd like to go six months before returning here.
P- had waited – oh, so long, that she just left
To come tomorrow to get shots which should have been today
And I felt guilty that I'd tried to see too many patients
Started up too late – and they all waited, waited, far too long today.
The lesions on the back on Mrs. M. had grown a bit –
We've almost run the gamut of the medicines which might apply
For her.
And so I started over just to see
If going back and trying once again would work.
Now Mr. M. was one bright spot – the node was almost gone
And so, I told him we would try to hold it there
With lesser medicines (I hope . . . oh how I hope . . . that it will work.)
F-'s breast was still enlarged a bit – and slightly red
Inflammatory change, I hope, and wish I could be sure.
And G- looked so weak and gray . . . so ill

He'd done so well for a few months – the mass had shrunk – then
Back it came again. His arms were numb – and x-rays once had shown
A lesion in his spine up in the neck – and quadriplegia might result
Though he is just so ill – in other ways – so jaundiced and so weak . . .
In spite of this, I called for help to treat his spine . . .
and know I'll be condemned
For not obtaining new x-rays before I sent him down.
(It was too late, today.)
His pain is better far – than it has been – that at the least is good.
And earlier . . . when Mr. T. came to call
To thank me for the things I'd tried to do to help his wife
His lovely, lovely wife
Who did so well for a few months – then faded – and expired
I feel a loss – I feel deprived. She was too beautiful and loved her life
Too much. And Mr. T. tries so hard to readjust and justify.
Then in the middle of the afternoon, the telephone –
And Mr. S. was dying at his home – the rescue squad was there –
They'd gotten him resuscitated a bit – and I inquired – For what?
The wife was yelling at the time: "I can't decide . . . I can't play God"
When she was asked just what she wished to do.
He died en route to Chippenham – or somewhere which was close.
Tonight, per phone, she tells me it was better as it was
And I agree. At least he did not die with children looking on.
And she seems reconciled a bit . . . and she will make it on her own.
One more this afternoon, a courtly gracious man
A black man – business man with much success – on Town Council, too,
I'd known a relative of his some years ago –
He kept repeating how he trusted me. I wish . . . oh how I wish . . .
That I could justify his trust and that of all these ones I want to help
But have so little which is valuable to give.

To Give the Soul its Chance
October 6, 1972

"You know," she said, as I got up to go, "I trust you more than anyone
Than any doctor that I've ever had (And I've had lots.)"
It was the sort of thing that Mrs. S. tried to say – although at
later date, much later in the course of her disease;
The latter lost her verbal aptitude and said, more haltingly,
"I've never had a close relationship with any one particularly – my
Mother was a sort of friend – not one on whom I leaned – for help
A different thing it is with you – a new experience –
I wanted you to know how much I care – how glad I am – you have
Concern for me."
The new one almost instantaneously
Extended heart – as well as hand – And I to her . . .
What was it that I felt?
I liked her – wanted her to live – to play that violin
To make the music that I cannot make myself.
I felt the tug of impotence – of knowing far too well
The limits of the art I practice "scientifically" . . .
I felt that massive liver – and I quailed
The odds I'd pictured in my mind before increased
I wished it were not so – I wanted to deny
The thing I felt – and had to own was real
I'd quoted Graham Greene already re: despair –
But that was not a needed thing
She came prepared to hope – And I prepared to give an honest hope –
But then . . . such pleasure was it to just listen to
Her reasoned comments re the role she knew she played
The "noble one" she really wasn't – so she said,
She only hated waste . . .
The waste, I hate, dear soul, I spoke unheard, is this:

The waste of this your life – not failure to employ
For useful purposes the bone and flesh which house
Your soul.
These transients – these cells this flesh which gives
Alike the power to manifest a soul and then to nullify.
And I? . . .
I chose to try to keep the cells alive to give the soul
Its chance.
With students I may try to give another thing – (This then the antidote)
I have an opportunity to work with heart as well as health –
And if my time were solely spent in fighting off decay, I might rebel
For building attitudes and widening minds is still a greater thing
Than keeping bodies here
The bodies that I try to save are those who need a chance
To share their souls.
Crusader
No. Mere supplicant – the one who stands beside and begs –
And fights – for life for you. Because without the light you have to give
Far poorer is the world.

Saving the Spark
September 27, 1968   11:45 P.M.

And I, too, ran . . . because I had already said goodbyes . . .
And anticlimax did it seem to go again
And if I thereby negate all the good I thought I did
All the concern I shared – then let it be . . .
For there are times, when saying once again
The obvious – becomes too much for you and also then
Too much
For me.
Ambivalent I will admit I am
I really find myself impelled
Into that room – and yet I ran – Before I should submit
To that desire to witness for myself
The current state – to look again into that face
Which looked into my own with trust – and who I failed
Though not for any lack of effort or, I think, of skill.
My role was that of optimist – in early days – in which
It seemed a chance – a full and pregnant likelihood
Still loomed – That we might salvage from the dregs
Of seeming sure defeat – a spark – which could be fanned
Some days – which could be stretched – to weeks – Or months.
And when that chance has faded, and responsibility
Belongs to others . . . not to me . . .
Then to withdraw should be the better part
Of valor.
And return . . . Mistake . . . Not kindly heart.
Can instincts then be trusted – or must I admit
I rationalize?
And as I wrote these words, the telepage
A summons issued . . . and the message was

"It is for you he asks just now . . . his wife and he
Expect you still to see them once again tonight."
Those instincts that I thought I read aright
But led me down a path
Interpreted at length – as that I wanted – but a wayward road
From that where duty led.
And so I went . . . and hand reached out
And eyes implored as throat unable was to find the volume
For the words. And I sedated, for there seemed no point
In summoning heroics at that time . . . And then I talked –
And held her hand . . . and tried to say some words which might impart
Some strength with which she could attempt
To meet the hours which lay ahead. And not the hours alone . . . but also
All these days and weeks – "No 'half-way' stuff will do," I said,
You must believe . . . that there is power in the universe –
And that we are a part of it. And if you say "Why me?"
you must be willing still to add: "Why not?"
And that which you had is dead already
In the sense that it cannot return in time. For it is now a part of you
And will be just as surely now – or more – than it had been before.
Thus on, and on, in hopes that one small phrase
Somehow might be the spark that set-the tinder into blaze . . .
I do not know that this I did achieve
Because for me to give a useful faith to yet another one
I also must believe . . .

SETBACKS

Don't Bring the Children
(no date)

Don't bring the children in again,
They can't see me like this –
A shadow of the mother that I was
In other days to them.
The little boy must never know
My legs won't move;
Why, only yesterday he stood by me
And lisped in childish innocence:
"We want you home again – and soon
To play with us,
Why, Daddy's fixed a swing;
And robins built their nest
Out by the shed;
And Sister's grown – she's almost big
Enough to play – at hide-and-seek
The way we used to do
When you were home."
My little ones can't understand
God knows I've tried to tell
That life for them must still go on –
Although I won't be there.

To Walk
September 16, 1977 10 P.M.

"If I could walk as you can walk", she said,
"I would not be so pessimistic and morose.
I would not lie here weeping bitter tears
And thinking of what might have been but has not been."
It was a trite response I gave – though true
"I wish with all my heart that you could walk . . .
You know I do . . . but it is mind and heart which counts
Not legs. And those you have . . ."
"I know that that is right," she said . . .
But I felt guilt
And she felt anger
That my legs support my weight
And hers jerk uselessly
Against the sheet.

Failed Grief
February 14, 1977

"We trusted you," he said, "And I must go on trusting you
And thinking that there was no other way . . .
But that last day I cannot yet forgive
Why did those doctors not know what to do?
Why did that nurse insist she take that pill
She could not swallow . . . Why did I
Go on home to leave her there
To die alone?
If I'd just known how bad things were
I would have stayed . . .
It's eating me – and I will never feel at peace
About it now . . . it will be with me on and on."
"You cannot feel that way," I said.
Although I, too,
Shall never feel I was immune from blame
I should have emphasized to you the risk
That she would not survive this time . . .
I could not bring myself to lay it cold
Upon the line – I still had hope
That we could salvage something once again
I didn't think that we would lose so soon,
Although I knew that it was possible.
I think I should have told you so
In no uncertain terms – or at the least,
I should have shared my fears
With you.
Two guilty souls but sharing guilt
For something which was really neither's fault
And yet we are condemned to live

Remembering... and knowing that
The image we had each assigned ourselves
Was blemished... tarnished in a few short hours
We would relieve – but now
Those hours can never be
Retrieved.
And Mr. B. had hardly left when then the telephone
With an announcement that another patient had died – a little lady I'd
Admitted just a week or two before...
who kept on getting worse – progressively.
An hour with the in-law while I waited for the daughter to arrive.
The woman chaplain, Mrs. T., sat there with me, too.
The daughter came... and through her tears, kept saying:
"If I'd brought her to you first..."
And I, aware I had done nothing for the woman, which had
helped. The only thing I did was just to hold the daughter in my arms
And let her vent her grief.
I would have done the same with Mr. B. had circumstances been right...
I should have let him make the trip...
"Grief-work" he needed
And I failed to give him opportunity.

To J:
July 25, 1972 12:30 A.M.

I tried, dear J-
But maybe not enough
Today it was too late – the strategems were naught
And even if I'd been there yesterday
It might have been to no use.
At least you didn't have to see
Your good looks go – or jaundice come
Or find yourself with bladder bag
Or wheelchair bound . . .
It might have happened thus – in spite of all
I'd hoped.
So B- was right – and I was wrong
I wonder how . . .
His horoscope – he says – black magic – voodoo stuff.
Or was it just that I deferred too long
To make the move –
To treat before it was – too late.
. . . I'll miss you J- so much
So very much. How could I fail – in spite of all these years . . .
I did not snatch you up in time before the jaws of death
The concrete roller jaws came crushing down . . .
And then tonight
Let's get it over quick, he said
And I stood by – no overt action did I take
And yet . . . I acquiesced, I know . . . by letting them
Cut down the useless drip . . .
But had it been a useful one – you would not now be gone
We would be plugging on – to try to make
Another day . . .

"We're not succeeding now," she said, "but Susan, thanks for all . . ."
And to her husband J- . . . "I'm sorry . . . just don't worry now."
And to the minister who made the pious speech
"I've been down on my knees and in my heart in prayer for you . . ."
She smiled with all the gusto that she always had and said:
"Well good for you!"
It was a matter of a few short hours
That you were still – not smiling – thanking people for their acts
Or thoughts or care . . . Your spirit never broke . . .
You won, you know, dear J- . . .
In spite of all . . .
In spite of all . . .

To P:
(no date)

Your eyes are open but they do not see
Me standing there beside
Nor do you hear me speak – tonight
You were too good – too gentle – too polite
Four years of watching – now this terminus
I didn't mean for it to end this way
(You know that too) –
Those days you raced in on your way to golf
Or during lunch – Examination done –
The way you stood before the mirror
To reknot your tie
Plump cheeks – the picture of a healthy man –
And I was proud –
So proud that I forgot to grieve
To recognize this day that would arrive
No purpose served –
To try to visualize a mode of death
When all was going well –
And we had upper hand –
Be glad we could not see this day –
Still unbelievable
How could I let it come to this?
Could I have somehow done another thing?
How little still we know –
We stupid would-be healers of the sick.

The Family of the Patient . . . Postlude
November 7, 1967

And to those who had faith in me
As we stood by the bedside
As we watched their loved one die . . .
A pledge:
That then, and now – and for eternity
I gave the best I had . . .
I left no stone unturned,
And yet I tried to know
When – that time came which marked the end of what I had to give
As the physician in the case . . .
And heralded the time
That I should take my place beside
The ones who stand
The ones who mourn . . .
For I was also at that moment one
To whom a loss occurred
And all the skill – the knowledge – that I claimed to have
Became a worthless pawn . . .
And I must suffer
Also as they did . . . But in a way
My guilt – my loss – was greater –
For they all
Had looked to me
And I had failed.

Serving All
February 24, 1975

There are some people – like the L-'s
Who think the world revolves
Around their needs or their desires.
They think it nothing to call strangers
Out of bed – at midnight
When the problem could as well have waited
'Til the dawn.
They think it nothing to ask favors which the
Rest of us
Would never dare.
And then use threats or drop the names
Of others they have managed to enmesh
In their own web.
Nor do they feel the need to show
Their gratitude
For they have none.
It was expected that the world would jump
When they so much as sneezed.
"Now you will have to help me get a bed
At MCV" he said,
As though he could –
The arrogance is quite appalling
Nor is it justified.
And furthermore, such people are so dumb –
They never seem to understand
The simplest things – they question
And dispute – and ask for help
While still expecting all the ducks to line
Up in a row for them – in their own way.

These things we must endure –
For we are servants of the crass as well as of
The meek.
And never let it come to pass
That I jump through their hoops more rapidly
Than those of all the little folk
Who need me too.

Feelings of Duty
August 8, 1974 12:30 A.M.

"My husband didn't come tonight", she said,
"He was enraged
To find I'd come into the hospital without
His bringing me – or knowing that I was.
He's been so angry at me since I have been sick
He says it's just because I keep on working
And that makes me worse.
I'm not the wife to him he thinks I ought to be
But I consider work a duty; sex is play;
And if the one or other has to go
It has to be the second not the first.
But then I tell myself that I'm unfair . . .
And that he's right when he feels sorry for himself
Because I'm sick . . . It has upset his life
As well as mine.
But I so badly need a little
Sympathy."
I thought of yesterday when that young woman sat
In purple dress, upon the table
Daubing eyes
With purple Kleenex . . . And when I came in
Protesting. "I'm so sorry that I cried . . .
I need a moment just to recollect myself
I've hurt and hurt so long– I'm just not sure
That I can stand it anymore.
My arm just will not move– I try to type
When it's supported in a sling, I can,
My fingers move; but I can't elevate my arm
It's swollen so– it aches and stabs until I think

That I will scream, sometimes."
"I know you cannot tell me what will happen,
And I've tried to hope – this whole long time;
I've tried to think we'd get the better of the thing . . .
But now, I can't be sure – and, furthermore,
I know you can't.
But I'll admit I sometimes wish that it would go
In one way or the other – it's not dying that I fear –
It's living like I am: or worse, perhaps,
And making life a misery for them – As well as me.
I watched my father die
With cancer of the neck: a lingering painful death;
I do not want to live the way he was."

She Just Fights On
(no date)

"She's just too bright", her husband said,
"Too much upstairs . . . She just fights on . . .
You know I have a cat
That hunts about . . . it caught a rabbit once,
And maimed it . . . but it wouldn't die
I watched and waited but it wouldn't die
I couldn't bring myself to kill it
Get it done . . .
I had to get a neighbor who came then
And killed the thing for me . . ."
This was the husband who had told me once
That he believed
In euthanasia
For this his wife . . . his cheerful, busy wife,
Whose mind and hands work on,
Although her cancer still is smoldering;
She moves again and now can sit
For the first time in months
She might progress to walking if we persevere . . .
But even if she never walked again
That steel-trap mind goes on
Those moving hands go on
Creating, fashioning, designing, copying
She lives a life more full than many souls,
Who run or walk
Whose prime endowment is their legs and not their
Brain.

And home she went today
To dwell beneath the roof of him
Who cannot kill a wounded rabbit, but who begs
That it might die to spare his pain
At watching it.

TRIUMPHS
♋

Rejoice
December 7, 1990

What words are there to catch a nuance of the day?
A call from an old patient of some 20 years:
"I know I'm doing well again – each morning I awake
And realize that I can drive my car – that I don't hurt . . .
I think of all those days that I was wheelchair bound.
They ask: 'What should you do when you know time is short?'
My answer is to recognize that ordinary things may be
The secret that you need. It is just doing them that
Makes my heart rejoice."
For she was saying that she did not need
To run around the world
Or buy the things she'd always wanted but not had
She found her joy in all the little things of life
The daily satisfactions of a measured world.
This is not true of everyone.
The key, no doubt, lies in
The joy one had in daily things, the pleasures of
The usual.
For those who never made their peace with their own lives
A threatened curtain is just one more thing
To prove that it has been "a dirty deal" the whole way through.
There is no great profundity in all of this
We die the way we lived – and are less apt to die
If we love life
And find it meaningful.

Rosary of Souls
December 31, 1974

"You know, to us in Petersburg," she said,
"You are a kind of saint.
We've watched our friends go off to you
And some came back, so much improved . . .
You gave them extra months and years, sometimes,
And always gave them something else –
Your dedication – and yourself."
"First, Mrs. S., then A-,
And Mrs. F., and C- . . .
I could go on and on."
"Those names you mention", I replied,
"Were all so wonderful . . ."
(And to myself I thought: Yes, it is these,
And others who are part of this my
Rosary . . . my rosary of souls who shared with me
Their fight for life, their faith, their confidence . . .
We trudged together down a road that led
Up to their deaths . . . But on the way
There were oases where we waited for a while
Refreshed, and strengthened, hopeful,
Hiding heads in sand; but glad for respite
On our way.
Thus on and on, today, tomorrow, and the next . . .
No saint am I but rather
Pilgrim
On a road which leads but to
Infinity.

A Dent Made
February 25, 1987

This week has had its triumphs and its lows
The miracles of J- and R-
The real improvement which they showed
In what looked like impossibles
I was amazed that J-'s gruesome mass
Could fade somewhat as it has done
It seemed resistant to the best that we could give
It was about the worst that I have ever seen
And it kept getting worse between the times that she was here
I felt a fraud when I agreed to try to treat
It did not really seem that anything would help.
And yet the almost – miracle – it has decreased
Although it has so far, so very far to go
It made me feel like less a charlatan
Because the most I had the day she came
Was just my feeling that there must be something done
That someone had to try.
And Mr. B.'s lung cancer – deemed "untreatable"
By most of those I know
And worse because the liver was just full of it
And it protruded like a cantaloupe.
And then to see the abdomen-down – almost flat
Was miracle. And he felt better – partly due to prednisone
The acid test will be the SMA – if it improved as liver size has done.
These things are most important though they may not last
Because they give the feeling that we can control
To some extent, at least, the damned crab.
They look to me. I promise I will try – and then –
So many times, at least, my hope was justified
I made a dent.

How great, how wonderful if it may be.
Some outcome better than the dent.
The low points were the feeling that I do not know
The things I should – that I am "out of date"
That it is hopeless to attempt to learn these newer things
That all my bright and youthful colleagues know so well.
This keeps on haunting me . . . that I may miss some leads
My hunches and my crazy treatment plans
May help as they have helped some "hopeless" patients now
But they were tailored for the case at hand
And leave no residue of scientific worth.
Someday . . . I keep on hoping . . . I will stumble on
Some plan which works – and can be verified – and used again
By others . . . and can lead – to some small piece of knowledge
Which might last – a while.
May I, like these my patients find in this our lives
Some hope.

Gifts to Pass Along
June 28, 1976

Three hundred miles I drove today –
And back again – for what?
For those few minutes that I took with him –
"She looks so good," the son of Mrs. W. enthused.
"We're just so happy with the way she's done."
"You're just so great," M- said, "I love you so" –
Her eyes filled up with tears . . .
And N- said: "Each day I thank my God
That I am here – and functioning –
The swollen leg is not much price to pay –
For life."
(And I am grateful too, each time I think
Of her – remembering her tears – six years ago)
"My daughter's only four," she'd said, "I did so want
To have the chance to bring her up – and now . . ."
"I guess we never really value life," I said,
"Unless it's threatened – then we know" –
This long parade went by today – and most
were doing well –
With this or that of strategies
A pinch of this – a touch of that –
Some plan – some expectation of success –
Why should I ever be unhappy with my life?
I who am blessed by having sometimes in my hands
Some gifts to pass along – to those whose need
Is overwhelming – desperate –
How very, very happy should I be.

Let Me Bring Joy
March 15, 1967

A score and greater years ago I wrote
Some words which sketched a dream –
A plan –
I found them yesterday and read amazed
"So many, many souls depend on me –
Their health – their hope – their joy . . ."
And thus I thought at Meredith in '41
And thus I find myself today –
My day's fulfillment of a sort – of all
These words implied.
And though my "cures" are few – and "life"
I give is short
God grant that the last mentioned of that trinity
Be mine to give
To hearts which sorrow – souls which mourn
Let me bring joy
Let me bring joy
To these for whom the light has dimmed
Let me remind them life has still a song
That there can be supplies of strength
To meet our woes with joy
That even death may be a triumph of a sort
That peace goes on and on and on and on . . .

The Life of Nature
October 14, 1972   1 A.M.

If will to die means wish for nothingness, what then of "will to live"?
It is the wish to know – to feel
The golden glow of life,
The empathy between two souls
The joy of work well done,
The looking up and out into the firmament
The reaching out for all the wonder that is hid
Beneath the epidermis of a leaf.
The morel in among the moss,
The lichens by the spring,
The taste of crisp green acorns,
Fox grapes, sour wild plums . . .
The very way the earth erodes beneath an overhang
Along a little stream.
These, these the things that make a heaven here
And golden streets in paradise a wilderness.
How foolish to absent oneself from source of strength
When it is there to take.
When blue jays scream and thrushes sing
Like pealing chapel bells . . .
When there is magic –
Somewhere . . . underneath a pine
Or beech
And souls may starve within these sterile walls.
How many of the "ghetto children"
Might be salvaged yet
If there were streams and woods in which they played,
If with the woodland were the gift to look
To feel

To take the magic that it has to give.
Beneath the leaves
Pipsissewa is hid
Wild ginger merely needs a loving squeeze
To share its scent.
And water-skaters glide somewhere suspended on
The atom of the air above the pool.
For somewhere in some place we have not found as yet
Is all of this I need – and desperately –
How foolish not to recognize
This truth . . .
The Stranger even made the step from nothingness
To peace
When from the window of his cell
He saw a star . . .

Admiration of Good
October 28, 1976

What does one say when someone's patient says:
"I have to tell you something now while I still live
Because it is important to me that you know.
My whole life long I've wanted to have someone I could make
My idol – someone that I wanted most to be alike
I never found that one until the day that I
Met you. And from that day, almost, I've felt that way
I wish I could be kind and loving as you are . . .
So many other people say the same . . . I've heard them in
The waiting room. They've never said one word which was
The least bit critical. They don't complain when waiting
For they seem to know
That when you see them you will concentrate
On them . . . You see, we really feel you care."
If I have any of the good you say, I said, it is because
I see so many people who, like you, are just so good, so brave,
It rubs off some. How can I think of giving less than you
When you endure so much . . . so wonderfully . . . so selflessly.
And then she told me of her son whose arm was crushed
When caught in a machine at work
"If such an accident just had to happen," he avowed
"I was a better one than some to have it happen to . . .
For I was strong – and others like my brother who were smaller
Might have lost a life – not just an arm.
And now it's fixed and will not happen to another one.
If you have two of anything, you can afford
To get along with one."
"That last is what he told me when I had my breast removed", she said,
And I kept telling him a breast was nothing by comparison.

You'd be amazed how well he gets along
With just one arm. He can split wood; and, sometimes, mornings
While we're still asleep, he'll had some pancakes made
When we get up. He works, you know, just like before."
I know, I said, all this is what I mean
When I avow that I just constantly stand by
In awe and admiration at
The glory that I find in you – and yours –
Whatever good I may possess is just so minimal
When I compare it with the strength, the pure nobility
Which I am privileged to see
In you.

The Gift
November 30, 1976

He grinned from ear to ear
As he brought in the thing –
A Christmas scene with Santa in a sleigh
A lake of broken mirror glass
A little wooden church –
A snowman and some scattered holly trees
"My wife is feeling better now," he said
"I have a bit of Christmas spirit, too –
We've really struggled all these months."
"They gave me just six weeks to live –
A year ago – almost"
She said today – "And now –
I drive my car and do the things I'd
Like –
They sent me home to die
With morphine round the clock
Until that day that Dr. P.
Sent me here."
I cross my fingers every day
for her –
I never know –
How many days we have like this –
Or whether when tomorrow comes
She will be weak and wan –
Again –
The miracle we have is ours
Today –
Let each tomorrow find its own.

THOUGHTS ON DEATH

♋

In Her Case
(No date)

Death – in her case – was merciful
It dulled her senses as the curtains drew,
And left her half-awake – asleep
Half-knowing, yet not asking why or where,
Reacting, yet not feeling need to be
A cog in the machinery of the world.
She knew her friends who came to call,
And half-conversed
Yet like as not a sentence broke in two
The hinder end forgot – and just as well.
Still, the depression which had ground its teeth
Into her soul until this respite came
Had flown – and left a calm morass.

The Flame of Life
October 26, 1968

And I, if I were to write a paper with the unlikely title of *Psycho—Social Aspects of Death*, what would I say? Perhaps in rhythm speech some words like these:
What can the living know of death as physical phenomenon?
For each of us until the heart has stopped remains "alive" . . .
And none can tell us what it is to "cease" . . .
But Death is more than that: For those to whom it comes with warning it
Is not a moment but an era . . . with its rites, its protocols
Though never really understood – and never grasped . . .
Initially there can be only unbelief . . . for it is alien ground,
But as the flame of life slow ebbs, a finger reaches out
To test that new estate; an ear inclines
To try to hear the music past that Door. The mind begins to readjust
Its sights . . . And those of us who watch can see
The fissure widen with the days . . . and that which once
Seemed unbelievable becomes more clearly viewed . . . until
Acceptance of the possible becomes reality.
This, still, is not a recognition of the ultimate –
That comes, in time, as pure fatigue – It is not worth the effort
That it takes to fan the flame . . . Or else – alternative approach
I do not wish to struggle on . . . For I have had
Enough . . .
A similar variety of evolution may occur
For those of us who stand beside . . .
In early days, we fight . . . we fume . . . we castigate
If it appears that he the dying one assents too soon . . .
We bring the bellows and we beat and blow . . .
Until we also reach a point at which the change occurs
And . . . gradual . . . or rapidly . . . as case may be . . .

We also recognize the limitations of our art . . . the fact that we
Are but a part of the Universe . . . and subject also to its laws
And all our wishes are but wind on air . . . And then,
If we are wise . . . We will allow
That human being in our care to take a peek
At Destiny . . .
And not deny . . .
His right to wonder
If he has not had enough of this – this world in which for him
The sunlight has become eclipsed . . . And dwelling in that artificial
Night of shadows is no ecstasy . . .
But this decision is his own . . . and we can but recognize . . .
Decision when it has been reached by him, if we are sure he made
It based upon an honest knowledge of the chances which exist
That shadows may be chased away – for even yet a while.
But then, because, for most, acceptance is ambivalent
And none of us are yet endowed with gift of prophecy
We play a double hand . . . We strive to leave a path
For Life . . . If Fate so orders – and we burn no bridges out . . .
And we who did not create cannot cause to end . . .
But we may be still Acolytes . . .
to add a dignity . . . to set the stage . . . for him who stars
In that his final drama we call Death.

Citizens of a New World
1950

You have become the citizens of a new world,
You to whom the doors of Death are close,
Your friends stand by and watch and cry a bit
But make their future plans without your help.
Secretly they wish the gulf would widen and the days
Be shortened, lest the dying take too long
And they themselves become too much a part
Of that strange world to which you now belong.
They talk among themselves in undertones and often with a sigh,
But when they speak to you they banter cheerily,
You wonder why they prate such reassuring words,
And yet must see the gradual decline,
Must see the strength ebb out, the flesh depart . . .
The medicines, you know, can't stem the tide;
They bring release from pain – a short release –
Until the next hour comes – no lasting good derives.
And yet that husband you had thought to love you so
Now seems content to stand and smile, while you
Remember in the other days when for a trivial ill,
The specialists were hurried in – all therapies were tried.
And when you say, so hopefully, "When I go home . . ."
And he half smiles and says, "Yes, soon, you must."
But he has never once advanced that promise first.
And though he comes each day and holds your hand,
A veil descends, a wall appears, between your souls
That means – though you must never once admit

You know the truth – that you and he
Are now no longer members of the same estate,
But he – for time unknown to anyone – belongs to Life
And you – he knows – must even within the year
Be part of Death.

The Living of Today
August 12, 1970

A few more days together for the two of them
A few good weeks –
Is this a valid aim?
When we all know that all the patchwork possible
Will never be enough.
A few good days – each day a miracle
Each day an extra bonus, stolen from
The very jaws of death.
What value can one place on these?
Each day an eternity
This day – this hour – this second are
The only ones of which
We can be sure.
Tomorrow?
Let tomorrow bring
Its graves, its crape . . .
Soon – soon enough – the pestilence.
Today? Rejoice . . . Be glad . . . Believe
That if tomorrow never came there would be value in
The living of today.
"I get up early in the mornings," this he said,
"It is the nicest time of day – the pretty part . . .
And evenings? Well, you know, I like them, too . . ."
For one who loves the day – the night
Who loves his life,
No sacrifice too great must be to find for him
A stretch of "pretty days."
Let those who dread the dawn not deny the right
Of him who loves each day to have

As many pleasant days as we can squeeze
From any source at all.
Why must my joy be mixed with guilt when I achieve,
Somehow an unexpected benefice?
To ride the crest may make the fall more deep –
When it must come . . . And yet . . .
The only moment we are guaranteed is NOW.

What to Say?
December 9, 1970

It was a sudden cry and unrelated to
The conversation which had been in progress at the time,
But through her lips – explosively – that question which had been
Suppressed – yet constantly a leaden weight – undoubtedly:
"Just tell me, am I now about to die? I do not want to die . . ."
At times like this, I have been known to say:
"We all will die…"
That statement constitutes admission of a known, yet leaves an open end.
But at that moment, such a blatant dodge was sacrilege
And any words I said were pedantry.
It was protection, succor, which she begged –
Was I to try to pawn philosophy – or falsehood – or
Admittance while I recommended that
She make her peace with God?
Not one of these solutions seemed appropriate.
And so I gathered her within my arms and spoke a truth:
"I have no such intention," This I said . . .
(A dodge again– for expectation was ignored.)
And then . . . to lighten up the atmosphere a bit, I chaffed:
"You and my husband's mother . . . for she always used to chide
Her son for driving rapidly, and say: 'I have unfinished business
Upon this earth.'
And I expect you'd like to echo just such words . . ."
A corny way, perhaps, for saying that I understood –
For I do understand – and we had crossed one bridge together
On the journey that we make.
She knows I am aware of all the fear she feels –
It has been verbalized – this much is good . . .
And by the fact that I did not deny – in clear-cut words –

Her right to fear –
I have not closed a door . . . I did not say:
"We know that you will die; but you must play the game
You must allow me to approach you as a child who can believe in storks,
And Santa Claus, and cabbages,
or any fancy story which his elders choose to tell."
I did not say that, yet the room remains
For her to seize such fiction if she should so choose . . .
For "Truth" as much as mass has relativity.

The Sleep
(no date)

"Doctor", she said, as half-awake
She smiled through swollen lids,
"Doctor, I'm so drowsy now – these days,
I'm half afraid
That someday I'll sleep on – and on –
And not awake."
I pressed her hand, and smiled,
And reassured –
That is the word we use,
You know,
When we admit alone but not to them
That death is not so merciful –
That for each one who sleeps away
Into Infinity,
A thousand battle with each day
Each hour –
A thousand watch the tissue
Melt away
From what were once robust and facile limbs,
A thousand watch the pallor creep
Into the face,
The lips grow white,
The abdomen distend,
The pain engulf,
The sleep give way
To final sleeplessness
Which watches helpless
While each step a pace,
Death marches closer from afar

A growing specter,
And the footsteps sound
Each day a little louder
Than before.
At times they fade away a bit
Obscured by other sounds,
Then louder from the quiet
Reappear –
Approach – close in –
Until to seek escape
Is vain; and senses dulled,
The coma creeps,
And makes the last few breaths
A little less
Than Hell.

Day's End
March 17, 1972

Don't flagellate yourselves by
Counting odds;
And then an end looms visible
But none of us can estimate
The days or years which will elapse
Before that end
Or even if the end will come from
That you fear –
I do not recommend that eyes be closed
And future days ignored
I merely say "Why torture yourselves now?"
The lesion you can see was there
Two months ago –
And little change occurred in 8 weeks' time –
Tomorrow still is yours.
How many days – I do not know –
But if we choose the best we can
Then do it – as we will –
Why lose all these todays
Of which we're sure –
While brooding over what may come to pass
Such anxious moments offer not reprieve
But maybe harm –
They may subtract from days – not add
And surely they subtract from quality
And that – the quality – of days
Is paramount to all.

Positively
October 24, 1975

She must have known that I was trying hard tonight–
But not succeeding – quite –
I did care; yet I found myself
Inclined to blame her that she was so sick –
Inclined to think that all the prayers and words
Affirmed her expectation that she would get worse
Instead of better – and that nothing which I did
Would be of any good.
I was inclined to think that if she had believed –
From the first day that she could beat the thing
It would have helped my medicines
They would have done more good
And now we may have passed a point at which
Return is much more difficult – if not impossible.
The little metal cross – the books by Vincent Peale –
All these attempts to indicate her positives
And all but merely evidence that all her attitudes
are negative.
That she is playing martyr – sufferer –
Unto the audience of all her friends
And now she cannot change her role again
It is too late. She must still satisfy their aims
She must get all the admiration for her bravery
In meeting death . . .
And that requires that death be met – not merely faced.

Caught in Clutch of Circumstance
September 21, 1968 4 P.M.

"For there are some," I said to him, "Who know how well to live."
"But few there are, a smaller group . . . who know also
The way to die."
A reddened lid, a few convulsive shakes, of massive shoulders
And he bowed his head . . . "She knew," he said, "And her great
Hope was that she might not be . . . a burden to the children . . .
Or to me."
"And that, her wish, was granted, and we have . . .
All this for which we may have
Gratitude."
But on last night, I was reminded of my role, for as I stood
And tapped her chest, she begged,
"Please hurry, for it is . . . . my family I want – in here –
Beside me . . . now."
Dismissal of a sort, I recognized. My job was almost finished
And the illness fell
Into its place as only one small part – Of a long life which had included
So much more.
And foremost though it may have been in all these latter days
My words, my medicines, the creed by which she lived –
Now at the last, these shrank – to insignificance,
Before that great reality – the only surety . . .
The transience of Life.
"She was confused. She mumbled on, on this and that," he said . . .
"She called the names of puppies we had had, so many years ago. She
Spoke as though . . . the children were still babies . . .
and her mother there."
I nodded . . . for it proved again that truth –
I recognized last night.

Perspective . . . supervenes . . .
"I am not really brave," the daughter said, "I see this many times . . .
But it is different now – it is my own – and that I am a nurse
Becomes no use. Though I suggested that we stop
The oxygen – The fluids – though I wanted this – And you agreed,
We stand here now – defenseless – and we wait . . ."
My hand I placed upon her shoulder . . . for it served
No purpose now for writing orders or for needling veins.
For we were human beings only
Caught
In clutch of circumstance.
And so – because her mother I had loved, admired . . .
Because I stood in awe at all the strength they manifest . . .
I had – once more – as on so many times before –
To try to give the only thing I had
A portion of myself.

Proof
October 13, 1970 2:30 A.M.

We talked all day about the dying patient and his needs
The panelists – each one of us – said words –
We meant them – I am sure – but they were words . . .
I left to come upon – by accident – a "dying patient" in
The waiting room . . .
This patient's dying is a lengthy thing – I see her once a month . . .
"My brother," she exclaimed, "they're working on him there."
"Could you find out and let us know what's happening now?
At six o'clock he was his hale and hearty self –
We had spaghetti – and he ate with us . . .
Then in his office had a pain and called himself for help."
I looked into the room and saw the man – a dying man –
Just kept alive by tubes – and respirator bags . . .
And the physicians who were tending him – just shook their heads
And one went with me out to see his folks
"I'm sorry." he intoned, "It looks as though he will expire now soon."
They wept and shook – the sister – and the patient's girlfriend
(Girlfriend only for some twenty years . . .)
Beside them stood the priest who'd come with them
The two of us
Endeavored to assuage their tears – to give them help –
"Just save him," begged the sister, "anything . . .
Which can be done – just do it now – right now."
"He's all I have – my only brother – and we were so close . . ."
The girlfriend sobbed and moaned:
"Why is it I must lose each thing I love? – Each single thing?
He cannot die . . . I love him far too much for that . . ."
A bit of hope . . . he once began to breathe – again – upon his own
It almost seemed – that he might live . . .

We raced the stretcher to the surgery . . . the blood vent pouring in . . .
They waited . . . and I went along to see my waiting patients
And to try – to buy a few more breaths – for them . . .
And when I came again – the end had come – the ruptured vessel could
Not be repaired.
He died – the brother of my patient who had been the one
Supposed to die – not him – the healthy one . . .
The sister spoke the words expected when she moaned
"Why could it not be me instead of him?"
Should I have said – in candid honest way,
Don't worry, for it won't be long . . . you'll join him there
Your days are numbered – no one knows it more
Than I . . . I would not say it then– nor will I
Say it when
Her days seem shorter – even than she knows . . .
My mission is to help men live – until they die – I cannot yet predict
Which one will die . . . just when . . .
The truth I tried to tell today – no God am I
To know the whys, the wherefores – or the whens . . .
If ever there were proof to bear this out –
This proof unfolded here before my eyes
Tonight.

A Reassuring Lie
March 2, 1973

He mopes, he groans,
He weeps
His mother adds her tears.
And pushes Valium –
She watched his father die
From cancer of the lung
And she expects
Her son to do the same,
In the same way –
The wife refuses to submit
So easily –
"Please tell him he can still improve," she begs –
(And she is right)
"He's using all the sedatives
As an escape."
(And once again she's right)
This man who begged to hear
"The truth"
Had neither stamina nor will
To face it straight.
His asking for "the truth"
Was begging me to tell
A reassuring lie –
He knew the truth –
He really hoped I'd offer him –
Some new alternative.
But that day was the one
I brazenly
Came out with …

And let him have the
Real, hard elemental whole.
The price I paid is dear –
Withdrawal – emesis –
The wish to sleep away the little life
Which may remain –
I understand –
Too well –
I stand amazed
Too many times
At those rare souls
Who can erect
Defenses – Cherish moments
Which may yet
Remain.

Don't Say Death
(no date)

Those who speak most
In self-assuring tones
Are those who fear it most.
Those who say oft
That they await
The muted call,
They are the ones
To whom it strikes
The deepest blow;
They tremble in their souls
Though on their line
They find the word:
Death.

A CAREER IN MEDICINE

To Leave What One has Loved
July 8, 1991

When all these things I do are all that I have done
For umpteen years, it is impossible – almost –
To think of walking out and leaving them.
Although someday . . . and someday soon, perhaps, this must be done.
Does anybody ever write a book about how difficult
It is to leave the things that one has loved?
Do those who revel in the joys of quitting work
Still find retirement is a happy time?
My problem is that there is still so much
I want to do.
I cannot bring myself to say that this is all
That I will ever do in this my role
I know that there are substitutes and newer roles
I wish I knew just what such days might bring
I wish that I could find the challenges
Which must be there . . .
I know that lack of pure self-discipline
May limit me
I know I am amoeba-like – and I react
To just the probing needle on the slide
Without that needle just what might I be?
I wish I knew.

Different Roles
May 31, 1975

When did that subtle change occur
When I gave up
Becoming a great clinician – chemist – scientist
When I acknowledged that my power to learn
Was limited.
And that I just could not compete
On the same grounds as those young ones
Surrounding me –
I've had the sublimation factors
Which could reassure –
That I had something – undefined
Which others lacked –
Perhaps it was just willingness
To spend more time –
And not some greater power
Of empathy –
But even if it were – it is not half
Enough.
To make up for a deficit in knowledge
Or in skill.
I pray I do not lack such now –
And that I give
The ones I treat the best of all
The "modern" knowledge usable and
Practical –
I know full well I haven't really "given up" –
I'm just still searching for a change
Of Roles.
Another basis for another try –

An area which will allow
For lesser energy and
Lesser strength –
I do not think I can compete
At tennis; but I might excel
At tic-tac-toe.

*Another Retirement Party**
July 21, 1983

They gave a party for me on this date – a farewell thing
J- presented me a vase and said nice things
And J- came.
And many of the people came to me
And said their thanks for what I'd done – or tried to do
There must have been some thirty people there – at least
PTs, OTs and nurses from the floor
And C-, P- and J-, some residents
A lot of food – and punch – and coffee and all that
It was surprise for me . . . I was not dressed for it
I'd even called to C- just before the thing
To cancel out the meeting that we often have
On Thursday at that time . . . He said he thought I'd better come
And told me what was going on . . . and so I went
And once again . . . I did the things I thought that I
Should do . . . I thanked them all for all their help
My speech was just a little wooden in my ears . . .
I'd stood there other times – for farewell parties
For the other staff – for J- the housekeeper, H-
For A- in her bright red dress.
I'd even put a hundred of my own and more into the pot
To buy her television set.
The things I said for her and for Ms. B.
Rang truer in my ears than all the things
I said for me.
But I do know . . . I kept this ship afloat
I raised the residents from one to six
I held the summer programs in a decent way
I kept the faculty together generally

I healed some wounds. I made Grand Rounds succeed
I even got the Training Grant award – the final coup . . .
What else is there to say . . . when all the time . . .
I kept all my commitments to the other things I do
I saw my patients, did attending stints, the Senate,
All of that. And J- emphasized again his gratitude
For what I'd done . . . he did not know I'd never been relieved
From any of the duties in the internal medicine and oncology world.
I'd had to do it all somehow . . . someway . . . how wonderful
If during all that time, I'd had one day just one –
To really be the Chairman. What a bliss it would have been
But torn by this and that – and pulled in many ways
I did a decent job – for that, at least,
I'm glad.

*Retirement as Acting Chairman of the Department of Rehabilitation Medicine, MCV

ON WRITING

Why Write?
February 10, 1974

Why write?
If not to gain acclaim
Why write?
If only for one's self?
What better reason
Could exist – than searching soul
Self-searching soul –
To ask the whys – the
Wherefores – and the what ifs?
What quirk possessed me, then,
To share?
Perhaps I needed to make
The points – and words –
Once written at a time when
Feeling was
Intense –
Conveyed a spirit that I
Could not
Grasp at will –
"When did you start to write?"
She asked –
"Was it at Meredith?"
No – not at Meredith
But long before – long, long
Before –

(Then, too, of course, but not
For other eyes)
No more than have there been
Words written since
For many eyes but mine –
But recently – when circumstances
Seemed appropriate –
My secret words I've used
With overwhelming praise –
At times
Perhaps they were emotional
To such a great degree
That they may have felt
As once I did
When some sad soul …
From Eugene Field –
I wept almost for Boy
Blue, the dusty toy dog
Just as they wept tonight.
But is that bad?
I do not know that it is
Either bad or good –
I only know my "yellow pages" serve a need
For me.

These Pitiful Words
November 13, 1972

No time to dream
To think –
To write the words
To celebrate those souls
Who were – whose lives touched mine
On to more souls –
To more pain-wracked bodies –
On to the seeking
In potions of magic
Why now, dear God was no extra time
Granted
To those who would feel
As they act –
Why not both?
If feeling deters me
From finding the potions
Then let me be robot –
Machine-product doer.
If moaning and moaning about those
Who die
Deters me from working
To keep them alive –
A curse on my thinking – my searching
My writing –
A mere self-indulgence
These pitiful words.

Too Many Things to Say
November 17, 1989

"How do you handle stress?" The rehab student asked
Her tape recorder rolling while our staff sat there . . .
And each of them came forth with pertinent remarks
"We share our problems," someone said,
"We know that we will lose the patient and we are prepared . . ."
"As long as we can feel we did the best we could, we are assured."
Another said . . . and on and on . . .
Each statement made was good
But I sat there and thought and did not say a word
There were too many things to say – and I have said them all
So many times
Too many times.
"It's not the patient care which gives us stress," said one,
It is the paper work – the picky things – the politics
And she was right.
Those things compound the patient generated stress
I hate, detest those people who are so afraid
Of "burn-out" that they never really glow
So self-protective that they never really give
I block on all of this – I adamantly refuse
To think that I could hurt myself by giving to those souls
Whose need is great.
And yet . . . I know that all the words I write
The pages and the pages I have written through the years
Were stress-induced – were easing pain
By writing as these words of now.
So many times they've been the balm . . . have brought the peace
The very typing and the rhythm of the words
They are to me my conversation with
The infinite.

Rope of Cancer
March 28, 1973

And in this life
If one lives long enough
And one's name is Susan Mellette
One comes to know many things
To walk on many floors
To know many tears and embraces
To share-- to live vicariously
In many climes.
Tonight a first . . . for
Who am I to feign to understand
Rope sculptures
Though they be
Creation of a woman by whose side I stood
The days before her mother died
A feeling woman who I cannot understand
Although I understood the love she had
For that most noble piece of pure humanity
Which bore her and who loved her then . . .
You see, I loved her mother, too,
Although I could not understand
The language that she spoke
I understood the feeling tone behind the words . . .
I tried to help-- I wanted to
So much I wanted to- but I could not . . .
Rope sculpture in the center of the floor there was tonight
Its title: *Cancer- Late Stage*;
Its substance tendrils, tentacles, brown, white here, black there
A mass of knots-- of matted rope
This I could understand.

As I could understand the hanging robes of gold and white
The formal treatment titled *Solitude*
That one created, Gilda said, to symbolize those months
Of her aloneness when her mother left our earth.
The artist lays his soul upon the line
Exposes all the inner core– the turmoil and the calm
And then is brave enough or brash enough to say
"Two years of my creative genius went here
In bits and pieces, it is true
But it was honest work.
Which way to twist this rope or that?
Which texture or which color here to use?
For this the thousand dollars that I ask
Is not mere justified but minimal …"
I stand amazed … how great humanity
That it may somehow recognize the novel ways
In which one says the things that one must say …
If clay or marble serve as medium
Then why not rope?
Tin cans or telegrams?
And why not for us mundane souls
Words.

Poetry
February 27, 1974

"I have a poem which is new," she said
"Not published yet – and called
'My Polish Love'
I'll send a copy on to you" –
"My thanks," I said –
And sighed –
A new creation have I every day –
Unpublished all –
And unsubmitted all –
I wonder what this dear sweet soul
Would say – if she should know –
The reason and reams of
Poetry – so called – I have –
I did not say – "I also write a bit"
I kept my lips shut tight –
(Except to smile and say –
"I'd like to read your poetry" –
And so I would)
I don't remember what I said
Acknowledging her poems –
I knew that I thought of sending one of mine
Which reads in part –
'For when one speaks in verses, oft as not,
He speaks his soul' –
But spreading out my words for all who come
Would be a crass commercial thing
Like dancing, naked, in the public square.

THE LEGACY OF DR. SUSAN MELLETTE

The effects of Dr. Mellette's life and career continue to be felt. Here are some testimonials to that fact, in her colleagues' own words.

In Memoriam

"Susan Mellette came to MCV in 1954 spending her entire career in attending cancer patients, providing hope, and sustaining their quality of life. She retired as Professor of Medicine and Rehabilitation Medicine in 1995. Most of us are unaware that Dr. Mellette joined MCV despite membership in a minority group that was subject to severe discrimination. Today, it is hard to conceive of women in medicine as a restricted minority, but when Susan began her career, admissions committees severely blocked the entry of women. Dr. Mellette eventually served on MCV's Admission Committee and, for the competitive presence of women today in medicine and their growing presence in academic medicine, we owe much to her efforts…She didn't hesitate to fight the shortsightedness of administrators or the victimization of her patients by cancer. This woman was a true hero and all of us owe her a debt for taking on a sick system that denied women their birthright. She warmly supported her patients as their friend and champion. In this period of political correctness and the increasing depersonalization of care, we need more healers like Susan Mellette: a vital force who didn't hesitate to explode against prejudice."

Contributed by Dr. William Regelson

In Memoriam article, Journal of Cancer Education, 2001:
"…for almost half a century she made outstanding and continuing contributions to cancer control. She had a tremendous impact on patients and colleagues at both local and national levels.

Began medical school at the University of Pennsylvania as one of their first female students but completed her medical degree at the University of Cincinnati in 1947 due to Peter's early church work.

The sites of Susan's postgraduate training were selected on the basis of the varying locations of Peter's theology work and subsequent graduate education, but her career interest in oncology was kindled primarily by her experiences on a cancer ward at the St. Barnabas Hospital in the Bronx. Recruited to MCV with her cancer research grant and was 'instrumental in the subsequent development of the school's cancer education, cancer research and cancer patient care programs. In 1960, she succeeded Dr. Leone as Director of the Division of Cancer Studies, an academic unit that was the forerunner of a future cancer center.'

Dr. Mellette's initial efforts included expanding and energizing a tumor clinic and a tumor board, developing a cancer research laboratory supported by both National Institutes of Health and American Cancer Society Grants and a cancer education program that led many medical students to choose oncology as a career.

She was essentially a one-person cancer center until a number of new faculty joined her to form a National Cancer Institute – designated cancer center in 1975. She was clinical coordinator for this cancer center from the time of its formation until the late 1980s. Her development of a wide range of coordinated and vital support services for the cancer patient led to a unique and truly multidisciplinary cancer rehab program in the early days of the cancer center. This became a national model for this innovative approach to the total care of the cancer patient.

Dr. Mellette became a role model in oncology for students, postgraduate trainees and her many colleagues, both in Richmond and nationwide. She was able to combine her expertise in patient care with an honest and palpable compassion for her patients and their families and a strong commitment to service for others. Susan and her late husband of almost 50 years, Peter, were a great team over both of their illustrious careers. The Drs. Mellette were devoted parents, despite their heavy load of responsibilities outside their home… Susan Mellette had a major impact on the lives of her loving family, her devoted patients and students, and her multitude of admiring friends and colleagues, She really did make a difference in the lives of many."

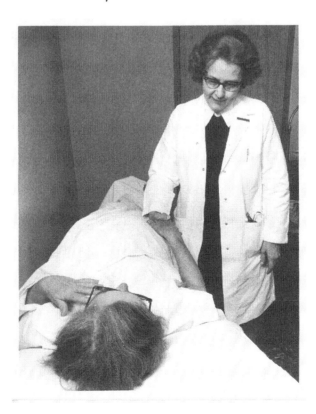

In PT Magazine, in 1998, Steve Gudas, PhD, PT mentions the impact of his mentor, Dr. Susan Mellette:

"My patients have taught me about life's grand cycle and not to be afraid of it," adds Gudas, who has devoted his 25-year career to oncology physical therapy. Currently, he is a faculty member at the Medical College of Virginia.

"What is hardest for me is parents with young children. At the times when my emotions threaten to take over what I am trying to do professionally, I call upon the advice of one of my mentors, Susan Mellette, MD: 'When faced with a situation in which your emotions are interfering with your clinical effectiveness, find something concrete that you can do.' I remember a situation like that. I was working with a woman who had young children, and her husband had already died. It bothered me terribly. I couldn't stop thinking about her having to die with such worry about who would take care of her children. Dr. Mellette advised me to find out what was going to happen to those children. I learned that arrangements had been made for this woman's sister to take her children, and that her sister was a caring woman who had children of her own and would provide a loving home for her sister's children. It was that one little concrete act that helped me deal with that situation."

Steve Gudas with Dr. Mellette at her retirement party

Dr. Mellette was also featured in news stories as well as the recipient of numerous awards during her career.

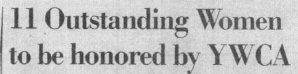

11 Outstanding Women to be honored by YWCA

By Cindy Creasy
Times-Dispatch staff writer

In the 100th anniversary year of the Richmond YWCA, 11 women have been named Outstanding Women of Greater Richmond.

The eighth annual awards were announced yesterday, but the women will be honored with a luncheon from noon to 2 p.m. Oct. 9 at the Richmond Marriott.

Tickets for the event are $22.50 per person and the proceeds will go to the Women's Advocacy Program, which offers assistance to victims of rape and domestic violence.

In addition to the traditional categories, a special centennial award was given. No recipient was named in the category of communications this year.

The 1987 honorees are:
SPECIAL CENTENNIAL AWARD: Elvira J. Moore has cared for her great-grandson since his birth. Now 16, Myshir Lound Turner has brain damage and cerebral palsy, and cannot walk or talk. Myshir attended Hickory Hill School, where Mrs. Moore heads fund-raising projects and is president of the Parent-Teacher Association. Mrs. Moore has no means and doesn't own or drive so she must depend on public transportation. Yet she remains an active member of her church and supplements her income by sewing.

COMMUNITY: Catherine J. McAuley, with five children from New York, established Hanover Little Theatre at Hanover three years ago, and continues to perform there with partners Nancy Kilgore. She has worked in regional theater as director and writer. She was in "Red, Hot and Cole," the music of Cole Porter.

Millie Jones began her Festival Flags, with a banner to hang outside her Fan home, to announce the birth of her daughter, she made colorful flags for weddings and family, and has

Northup   Cunningham   Capers   Moore

McAuley   Jones   Binford   Throckmorton

Mellette   Abbey   Rosi

expanded her one-woman business to 17 full-time and four part-time employees. She also volunteers for several Richmond organizations and has an interest in historic preservation.

EDUCATION: Dr. Virgie M. Binford has been a source of strength and support as essential in working with families in which a member is facing cancer. "There are not enough medals or honors to bestow on this lady—she has done so much for cancer victims and their families." This was the comment of one who has had occasion to observe her over an extended period of time.

Mrs. S., for example, recently has been diagnosed with breast cancer and a mastectomy recommended. Before her surgery, she was visited by Ms. Mary Scott, RPT, the program physical therapist, who evaluated her and outlined a post-operative exercise program to assure good continuing function. She was also seen by Ms.

ents of pupils in kindergarten through third grade so they can help boost their children's academic performance.

GOVERNMENT/POLITICS: Lillian C. Throckmorton has been active

MCV Names Dr. Millette Director

Dr. Susan J. Mellette, who has been on the Medical College of Virginia staff since 1954, has been named director of the division of cancer studies at MCV.

Since February, 1961, she has been co-director of the division with Dr. William R. Nelson. Dr. Nelson resigned in July to resume private practice in Denver.

Dr. Mellette's appointment was made during last Friday's board of visitors meeting at MCV. The board also promoted Dr. Mellette to assistant professor of medicine. She had been assistant professor of research in the department of medicine.

Functions Listed

The division of cancer studies is composed of the tumor clinic and the tumor registry (where all records of patients with malignant tumors are kept). It also co-ordinates MCV's various cancer activities.

A native of Raleigh, N. C., Dr. Mellette attended medical school at the University of Pennsylvania and the University of Cincinnati.

Her husband, Dr. Peter Mellette, is executive director for Virginia of the National Conference of Christians and Jews.

Cancer in Virginia
The Greatest Fight of Our Lifetime

Massey Cancer Center

Summer 1987   Medical College of Virginia/Virginia Commonwealth University

Battle Lines in the Fight Against Cancer

Treatment for cancer at the new Oncology Clinic/Massey Cancer Center means state-of-the-art medical techniques PLUS concern for the whole person and the cancer patient's total life situation, which may be affected by the disease or its treatment, is considered as part of the therapy plan. Physical, psychosocial, and vocational rehabilitation may be needed along with emotional support for both the patient and the family in addition to the direct cancer treatment. This is the mission of the Cancer Rehabilitation and Continuing Care Program (CRCCP) directed by Dr. Susan J. Mellette.

Dr. Mellette is well-known nationally and internationally for her leadership in the field of cancer rehabilitation and cancer education. Her name and picture will be recognized by many who receive this publication as a person who has been a source of

Dr. Susan J. Mellette, director of the Cancer Rehabilitation Program at the Massey Cancer Center, and professor of internal medicine and rehabilitation medicine, Medical College of Virginia/Virginia Commonwealth University.

Judith Keziel, M.S., a rehabilitation counselor and coordinator of the CRCCP Breast Team, to determine whether any emotional or other concerns might affect her return to her usual activities and daily living routine. The team will continue to follow her until her rehabilitation is complete.

It is a Wednesday morning in the Oncology Clinic, and the clinic is filled with children coming in for their regular cancer treatments. Rev. Andy Puckett, the chaplain counselor, is talking with parents about any problems they may have encountered in connection with the disease or the treatment. Rev. Puckett's work is

funded by the Association for the Study of Childhood Cancer (ASK). At the same time, in the Cancer Rehabilitation OT/PT Treatment Room, a whole group of children seem oblivious to their parents and their treatments. They all in a circle, playing with xylophones and other musical instruments. The music therapist, Ms. Martha Bellamy, RMT, leads them as they sing together, taking their minds off their ongoing treatments and improving their emotional well-being. Music therapy is a recent addition to the services provided by the CRCCP and was made

Continued on page 6

Monarchs Meet a Mouse

MELLETTE

M. Susan Jackson Mellette, M.D., 78, departed this life September 10, 2000. A native of Raleigh, North Carolina, Dr. Mellette was graduated from Meredith College and received her M.D. from the University of Cincinnati. Her postgraduate training included residencies at Cleveland City Hospital, at St. Barnabas Hospital in New York, and at Koch Hospital in St. Louis before coming to Richmond in 1954. Dr. Mellette rose through the ranks at the Medical College of Virginia (MCV) to become Professor of Internal Medicine and Rehabilitation Medicine before becoming Professor Emerita in 1992 and retiring in 1995. She was a tireless pioneer and caring physician in the treatment of cancer patients using chemotherapy and was responsible for the development of the Cancer Rehabilitation and Continuing Care Program at MCV Hospitals that has helped thousands of patients on the road to recovery. Her many accolades include: AOA, Who's Who in America, Distinguished Medical Faculty Award, MCV Alumni Association, MCV Dean's Award for Community Service, Greater Richmond YWCA Woman of the Year in Science and Medicine, Professional of the Year, several American Cancer Society awards, and the National Brotherhood-Sisterhood Award from the National Conference of Christians and Jews, an award which she shared with her beloved deceased husband, Dr. Peter Mellette. In addition to patient care, teaching and research duties at MCV, Dr. Mellette also served as an officer or member of numerous hospital, local, state and national committees, including the MCV Admissions Committee, as President of the VCU Faculty Senate, several NIH peer review committees, as President of the American Association for Cancer Education, and as a member of the Advisory Committee on Hospice and of the Subcommittee on Terminal Care to the Virginia General Assembly. Dr. Mellette is survived by a daughter, Mrs. Susan M. Lederhouse of Orleans, Mass.; a son, Peter M. Mellette; a sister, Elizabeth Middleton of St. Johnsbury, Vt.; and two grandchildren, Kelsey and Margot Mellette of Williamsburg. Va. A memorial service is scheduled for 2 p.m. on Thursday, September 21, 2000 at the MCV Health Sciences Center auditorium, 1215 E. Marshall St. In lieu of flowers, kindly make memorial gifts to either the Susan Mellette Fellowship and Scholarship Fund (for medical students interested in oncology careers) of the MCV Foundation, P.O. Box 980234, Richmond, Va. 23198, or to the Mull-Jackson-Mellette First Family Scholarship Fund (for undergraduate students interested in science careers) at Meredith College, 3800 Hillsborough St., Raleigh, N.C. 27607-5298.

Cancer care pioneer dies at 78

BY ELLEN ROBERTSON
TIMES-DISPATCH STAFF WRITER

To her cancer patients, Dr. Mary Susan Jackson Mellette was the "angel" who battled beside them, walked the hospital floors at night to comfort them in the midnights of their fears, refused to give up the hope of making their lives better and often worked miracles.

The realization of Dr. Mellette, an oncologist, that the needs of cancer patients went far beyond physical issues led to a revolutionary change in patient care nationwide. She died of respiratory problems Sunday in a local hospital. She was 78 and lived in Richmond.

Her first exposure to cancer patients came during a residency in New York, where she saw "people being warehoused to die," said her son, Peter Mason Mellette of Williamsburg.

"She thought it was wrong, that there needed to be a better way of taking care of patients," he said. That exposure and the dark poetry she wrote about it crystallized her career.

She came to Richmond in 1954, bringing a research grant with her to Medical College of Virginia, where she joined the medical faculty in 1955.

SEE **MELLETTE**, PAGE B7 ▶

A Celebration of the Life of

M. Susan Jackson Mellette, M.D.
June 4, 1922 — September 10, 2000

Medical Sciences Auditorium
Medical College of Virginia
September 21, 2000
2:00 p.m.

SCHOLARSHIPS IN HONOR OF DR. MELLETTE

As a student, parent and long-time medical school admissions committee member, Dr. Mellette was particularly concerned about the escalating cost of education and its effect on career choice. During her lifetime, she established endowed scholarships for undergraduate and medical students at her alma maters (Meredith College and the University of Cincinnati) and at the Medical College of Virginia Foundation/VCU.

At Meredith College, the Mull-Jackson-Mellette First Family Scholarship, named for Dr. Mellette as well as her alumnae mother and sister, awards scholarships annually to students interested in the health sciences.

Through the Susan Mellette Scholarship Fund held at the MCV Foundation, medical students receive scholarships based on their interest in oncology and any established activities or studies that support this interest.

The net proceeds from book sales will go toward funding these scholarships.

ABOUT THIS BOOK:

Dr. Susan Mellette wrote these poems longhand or typed them in her office at MCV. She wrote at least 550 poems that were later transcribed by her son Peter Mellette, with the help of Laura Safley. All of the poems and journals could not be featured in this book, but those selected are representative of her writing.

Made in the USA
Charleston, SC
09 June 2015